Please indicate the titles you would like:

Romeo and Juliet   1.65   _1.65_

Jane Eyre   4.25   _____

Frankenstein   2.50   _____

Illustrated Man   9.10   _____

To Kill a Mockingbird   7.90   _____

# of books ordered: _1_   Total: _1.65_
($25.40 for all five books/ not all books have to be ordered)

Name: _Stefan Frick_   Section: _03_

Table of Contents

Strategies for Understanding Shakespeare's Language

1. **When reading verse, note the appropriate phrasing and intonation.**

   DO NOT PAUSE AT THE END OF A LINE unless there is a mark of punctuation. Shakespearean verse has a rhythm of its own, and once a reader gets used to it, the rhythm becomes very natural to speak in and read. Beginning readers often find it helpful to read a short pause at a comma and a long pause for a period, colon, semicolon, dash, or question mark.

   Here's an example from *The Merchant of Venice*, Act IV, Scene i:

   The quality of mercy is not strain'd, (*short pause*)
   It droppeth as the gentle rain from heaven
   Upon the place beneath: (*long pause*) it is twice blest; (*long pause*)
   It blesseth him that gives, (*short pause*) and him that takes; (*long pause*)
   'Tis mightiest in the mighties; (*long pause*) it becomes
   The throned monarch better than his crown; (*long pause*)

2. **Reading from punctuation mark to punctuation mark for meaning.**

   In addition to helping you read aloud, punctuation marks define units of thought. Try to understand each unit as you read, keeping in mind that periods, colons, semicolons, and question marks signal the end of a thought. Here's an example from *The Taming of the Shrew*:

   > Luc. Tranio, I saw her coral lips to move,
   >   And with her breath she did perfume the air;
   >   Sacred, and sweet, was all I saw in her.
   > Tra. Nay, then, 't is time to stir him from his
   >   trance.
   >   I pray, awake, sir: if you love the maid,
   >   Bend thoughts and wits to achieve her. (I,i)

   The first unit of thought is from "Tranio" to "air":
   He saw her lips move, and her breath perfumed the air.
   The second thought ("Sacred, and sweet...") re-emphasizes the first.

   Tranio replies that Lucentio needs to awaken from his trance and try to win "the maid." These two sentences can be considered one unit of thought.

3. In an **inverted sentence**, the verb comes before the subject. Some lines will be easier to understand if you put the subject first and reword the sentence.

For example, look at the line below:

"Never was seen so black a day as this:" (*Romeo and Juliet, IV, v*)

You can change its inverted pattern so it is more easily understood:

"A day as black as this was never seen:"

4. An **ellipsis** occurs when a word or phrase is left out. In *Romeo and Juliet*, Benvolio asks Romeo's father and mother if they know the problem that is bothering their son. Romeo's father answers:

    "I neither know it nor can learn of him" (*Romeo and Juliet I,i*).

    This sentence can easily be understood to mean,

    "I neither know [the cause of] it,
    nor can [I] learn [about it from] him."

5. As you read longer speeches, keep track of the subject, verb, and object – *who* did *what* to *whom*.

    In the clauses below, note the subject, verbs, and objects.

    Ross: The king hath happily received, Macbeth,
        The news of thy success: and when he reads
        Thy personal venture in the rebel's fight... (*Macbeth I, iii*)

    1st clause: *The king hath happily received, Macbeth,/The news of thy success:*
    SUBJECT – The king
    VERB – has received
    OBJECT – the news [of Macbeth's success]
    2nd clause: *and when he reads/thy personal venture in the rebel's fight,*

    SUBJECT – he [the king]
        VERB – reads
        OBJECT – [about] your venture

    In addition to following the subject, verb, and object of a clause, you also need to track pronoun references. In the following soliloquy Romeo, who is madly in love with Juliet, secretly observes her as she steps out on her balcony. To help you keep track of the pronoun references, we've made margin notes. (Note that the feminine pronoun sometimes refers to Juliet, but sometimes does not.)

5

But, soft! what light through yonder window breaks?
It is the east, and Juliet is the sun!
Arise, fair sun, and kill the envious moon,
Who* is already sick and pale with grief,   *"Who" refers to the moon.
That thou her* maid art more fair than she:*   *"thou her maid" refers to Juliet,
                                                                              the sun.
                                                                      *"she" and "her" refer to the moon.

In tracking the line of action in a passage, it is useful to identify the main thoughts that are being expressed and paraphrase them. Note the following passage in which Hamlet expresses his feelings about the death of his father and the remarriage of his mother:

> O God! a beast that wants discourse of reason
> Would have mourn'd longer – married with my uncle,
> My father's brother, but no more like my father
> Than I to Hercules. (I,ii)

Paraphrasing the three main points, we find that Hamlet is saying:

- a mindless beast would have mourned the death of its mate longer than my mother did
- she married my uncle, my father's brother
- my uncle is not at all like my father

If you are having trouble understanding Shakespeare, the first rule is to read it out loud, just as an actor rehearsing would have to do. That will help you understand how one thought is connected to another.

6. Shakespeare frequently uses metaphor to illustrate an idea in a unique way. Pay careful attention to the two dissimilar objects or ideas being compared. In *Macbeth*, Duncan, the king says:
> I have begun to plant thee, and will labour
> To make thee full of growing. (I,v)

The king compares Macbeth to a tree he can plant and watch grow.

7. An *allusion* is a reference to some event, person, place, or artistic work, not directly explained or discussed by the writer; it relies on the reader's familiarity with the item referred to. Allusion is a quick way of conveying information or presenting an image. In the following lines, Romeo alludes to Diana, goddess of the hunt and of chastity, and to Cupid's arrow (love).

> ROMEO: Well, in that hit you miss: she'll not be hit
>   with Cupid's arrow, she hath Dian's wit;
>   and in strong proof of chastity well arm'd (I,i)

8. Contracted words are words in which a letter has been left out. Some that frequently appear:

be't	on't	wi'
do't	t'	'sblood
'gainst	ta'en	i'
'tis	e'en	
'bout	know'st	'twill
ne'er	o'	o'er

9. Archaic, obsolete and familiar words with unfamiliar definitions may also cause problems.

- **Archaic Words** Some archaic words, like *thee, thou, thy*, and *thine,* are instantly understandable, while others, like *betwixt,* cause a momentary pause.
- **Obsolete Words** If it were not for the notes in a Shakespeare text, obsolete words could be a problem; words like "beteem" are usually not found in student dictionaries. In these situations, however, a quick glance at the book's notes will solve the problem.
- **Familiar Words with Unfamiliar Definitions** Another problem is those familiar words whose definitions have changed. Because readers think they know the word, they do not check the notes. For example, in this comment from *Much Ado About Nothing*, the word *an* means *if*:
  > **Beatrice:** Scratching could not make it worse, *an* 'twere such a face as yours were. (I,i)

  For this kind of word, we have included margin notes.

10. Wordplay: puns, double entendres, and malapropisms

- A *pun* is a literary device that achieves humor or emphasis by playing on ambiguities. Two distinct meanings are suggested either by the same word or by two similar-sounding words.
- A *double entendre* is a kind of pun in which a word or phrase has a second, usually sexual, meaning.
- A *malapropism* occurs when a character mistakenly uses a word that he or she has confused with another word. In *Romeo and Juliet*, the Nurse tells Romeo that she needs to have a "confidence" with him, when she should have said "conference." Mockingly, Benvolio then says she probably will "indite" (rather than "invite") Romeo to dinner.

Reading Pointers for Sharper Insights

As you read, look for the themes and elements described below.

- **Courtly love**: This term describes a set of attitudes and rules that originally governed courtship among upper-class citizens of Europe in the Middle Ages. Certain patterns of courtly love lasted into the literature of the Renaissance; they appear in Shakespeare's sonnets as well as this play. Standard topics of courtly love include the following:

  1. The idealization of the beloved, especially through images of light and dark:

     ROMEO: But, soft! what light through yonder window breaks?
     It is the east, and Juliet is the sun.
     Arise, fair sun, and kill the envious moon,
     Who is already sick and pale with grief,
     That thou her maid art far more fair than she…
     II.i.4-6

  2. The agony of the lover—he or she cannot live without the beloved:

     ROMEO: 'Tis torture, and not mercy: heaven is here,
     Where Juliet lives; and every cat and dog
     And little mouse, every unworthy thing,
     Live here in heaven and may look on her;
     But Romeo may not…
     III.iii.29-33

  3. The emphasis on innocence and purity, especially when contrasted with more "worldly" love affairs. Unlike the Nurse, whose language is bold and suggestive, Juliet thinks of love as "holy," and discusses it in terms of saints and pilgrims in her conversations with Romeo.

- **Fate**: The Prologue tells the reader that in the play, "A pair of star-crossed lovers take their life." Fate is a powerful force in *Romeo and Juliet*, and the main characters are highly aware of it. Romeo, for instance, has premonitions of his own death several times.

- **Social conflict**: Contrasting with the idea that the young lovers are destined to die is a protest against the cycle of violence that leads to their tragic ends. Verona is the place "where civil blood makes civil hands unclean." The play opens with a brawl between servants of the two households, and reaches its climax when in a bloody duel that leaves members of both families dead. In the final act, the Prince sadly remarks upon the death of the young people by saying that the inter-family violence was bound to have terrible consequences.

  Because of the long history of hostility between the two families, Romeo and Juliet suffer intense pressure. The conflict between individuals and the larger groups of which they are a part (family, church, citizenry) is another important element in the play.

- **Language and poetry**: This is one of Shakespeare's early plays, but we can already see in it his fascination with language and the meaning of words. Juliet wonders about the arbitrary power of words when she asks why Romeo's name must keep him away from her. Other characters trick and tease one another with puns and wordplay.

DRAMATIS PERSONAE

Chorus.
Escalus, Prince of Verona.
Paris, a young nobleman, kinsman to the Prince.
Montague, head of one house, at odds with Capulets.
Capulet, head of one house, at odds with Montagues.
An old Man, of the Capulet family.
Romeo, son to Montague.
Tybalt, nephew to Lady Capulet.
Mercutio, kinsman to the Prince and friend to Romeo.
Benvolio, nephew to Montague, and friend to Romeo
Tybalt, nephew to Lady Capulet.
Friar Laurence, a Franciscan.
Friar John, a Franciscan.
Balthasar, servant to Romeo.
Abram, servant to Montague.
Sampson, servant to Capulet.
Gregory, servant to Capulet.
Peter, servant to Juliet's Nurse.
An Apothecary.
Three Musicians.
An Officer.
Lady Montague, wife to Montague.
Lady Capulet, wife to Capulet.
Juliet, daughter to Capulet.
Nurse to Juliet.
Citizens of Verona; Gentlemen and Gentlewomen of both houses;
Maskers, Torchbearers, Pages, Guards, Watchmen, Servants, and
Attendants.

THE PROLOGUE

SCENE—VERONA; Mantua.

Enter Chorus.

CHOR: Two households, both alike in dignity,
In fair Verona, where we lay our scene,
From ancient grudge break to new mutiny,
Where civil blood makes civil hands unclean.
5   From forth the fatal loins of these two foes
A pair of star-cross'd lovers take their life;
Whose misadventur'd piteous overthrows
Doth, with their death, bury their parents' strife.
The fearful passage of their death-mark'd love,
10   And the continuance of their parents' rage,
Which, but their children's end, naught could remove,
Is now the two hours' traffic of our stage;
The which if you with patient ears attend,
What here shall miss, our toil shall strive to mend.

Exit.

ACT I

SCENE I
Verona. A public place.

Enter Sampson and Gregory with swords and bucklers of the house of Capulet.

SAMP: Gregory, on my word, we'll not carry coals.[1]
GREG: No, for then we should be colliers.
SAMP: I mean, an we be in choler, we'll draw.
GREG: Ay, while you live, draw your neck out of the collar.
5 SAMP: I strike quickly, being moved.
GREG: But thou art not quickly moved to strike.
SAMP: A dog of the house of Montague moves me.
GREG: To move is to stir, and to be valiant is to stand.
　　　Therefore, if thou art moved, thou runn'st away.
10 SAMP: A dog of that house shall move me to stand. I will
　　　take the wall of any man or maid of Montague's.
GREG: That shows thee a weak slave; for the weakest goes to
　　　the wall.
SAMP: 'Tis true; and therefore women, being the weaker
15 vessels, are ever thrust to the wall. Therefore I will push
　　　Montague's men from the wall and thrust his maids to
　　　the wall.
GREG: The quarrel is between our masters and us their men.
SAMP: 'Tis all one. I will show myself a tyrant. When I have
20 fought with the men, I will be civil[2] with the maids; I will
　　　cut off their heads.
GREG: The heads of the maids?
SAMP: Ay, the heads of the maids, or their maidenheads. Take
　　　it in what sense thou wilt.
25 GREG: They must take it in sense that feel it.

[1] *tolerate insults [To carry coals was to perform the most menial household work that could be assigned to a servant; thus, it would be an insult or a source of humiliation.]*

[2] *"cruel" appears in some texts*

SAMP: Me they shall feel while I am able to stand; and 'tis
known, I am a pretty piece of flesh.

GREG: 'Tis well thou art not fish; if thou hadst, thou hadst
been poor-John.³ Draw thy tool! Here comes two of the
30   house of Montagues.

Enter two other Servingmen, Abram and Balthasar.

SAMP: My naked weapon is out. Quarrel! I will back thee.

GREG: How? turn thy back and run?

SAMP: Fear me not.

GREG: No, marry. I fear thee!

35 SAMP: Let us take the law of our sides; let them begin.

GREG: I will frown as I pass by, and let them take it as they
list.

SAMP: Nay, as they dare. I will bite my thumb at them;
which is a disgrace to them, if they bear it.

40 ABR: Do you bite your thumb⁴ at us, sir?

SAMP: I do bite my thumb, sir.

ABR: Do you bite your thumb at us, sir?

SAMP: *Aside to Gregory.*   Is the law of our side, if I say ay?

GREG: *Aside to Sampson.*   No.

45 SAMP: No, sir, I do not bite my thumb at you, sir; but I bite
my thumb, sir.

GREG: Do you quarrel, sir?

ABR: Quarrel, sir? No, sir.

SAMP: But if you do, sir, I am for you. I serve as good a
50   man as you.

ABR: No better.

SAMP: Well, sir.

Enter Benvolio.

GREG: *Aside to Sampson.*   Say 'better.' Here comes one of
my master's kinsmen.

55 SAMP: Yes, better, sir.

ABR: You lie.

SAMP: Draw, if you be men. Gregory, remember thy swash-
ing⁵ blow.   *They fight.*

BEN: Part, fools!   *He beats down their swords.*
60   Put up your swords. You know not what you do.

³*a cheap, salted fish*

⁴*[a gesture of contempt]*

⁵*smashing*

Enter Tybalt.

TYB: What, art thou drawn among these heartless hinds?[6]
    Turn thee, Benvolio! look upon thy death.

                                                 [6]hounds

BEN: I do but keep the peace. Put up thy sword,
    Or manage it to part these men with me.

65 TYB: What, drawn, and talk of peace? I hate the word
    As I hate hell, all Montagues, and thee.
    Have at thee, coward!   *They fight.*

*Enter an officer, followers of both houses, and three or four
Citizens with clubs or partisans.*

CITIZENS: Clubs, bills, and partisans![7] Strike! beat them
    down! Down with the Capulets! Down with the
70   Montagues!

                                                 [7]battle axes

Enter Old Capulet in his gown, and his Wife.

CAP: What noise is this? Give me my long sword, ho!
WIFE: A crutch, a crutch! Why call you for a sword?
CAP: My sword, I say! Old Montague is come
    And flourishes his blade in spite of me.

Enter Old Montague and his Wife.

75 MON: Thou villain Capulet!—Hold me not, let me go.
M. WIFE: Thou shalt not stir one foot to seek a foe.

Enter Prince Escalus, with his Train.

PRINCE: Rebellious subjects, enemies to peace,
    Profaners of this neighbour-stained[8] steel—
    Will they not hear? What, ho! you men, you beasts,

                                                 *[8]stained with a
neighbor's blood*

80   That quench the fire of your pernicious rage
    With purple fountains issuing from your veins!
    On pain of torture, from those bloody hands
    Throw your mistempered weapons to the ground
    And hear the sentence of your moved Prince.
85   Three civil brawls, bred of an airy[9] word

                                                 [9]trivial; unimportant

By thee, old Capulet, and Montague,
Have thrice disturb'd the quiet of our streets
And made Verona's ancient citizens
Cast by[10] their grave beseeming[11] ornaments
90   To wield old partisans, in hands as old,
Canker'd[12] with peace, to part your canker'd hate.
If ever you disturb our streets again,
Your lives shall pay the forfeit of the peace.
For this time all the rest depart away.
95   You, Capulet, shall go along with me;
And, Montague, come you this afternoon,
To know our farther pleasure in this case,
To old Freetown, our common judgment place.
Once more, on pain of death, all men depart.

Exeunt all but Montague, his Wife, and Benvolio.

100   MON: Who set this ancient quarrel new abroach?
Speak, nephew, were you by when it began?
BEN: Here were the servants of your adversary
And yours, close fighting ere I did approach.
I drew to part them. In the instant came
105   The fiery Tybalt, with his sword prepar'd;
Which, as he breath'd defiance to my ears,
He swung about his head and cut the winds,
Who, nothing hurt withal, hiss'd him in scorn.
While we were interchanging thrusts and blows,
110   Came more and more, and fought on part and part,
Till the Prince came, who parted either part.
M. WIFE: O, where is Romeo? Saw you him to-day?
Right glad I am he was not at this fray.[13]
BEN: Madam, an hour before the worshipp'd sun
115   Peer'd forth the golden window of the East,
A troubled mind drave[14] me to walk abroad;
Where, underneath the grove of sycamore
That westward rooteth from the city's side,
So early walking did I see your son.
120   Towards him I made; but he was ware of me
And stole into the covert of the wood.
I, measuring his affections by my own,

---

[10]*away*

[11]*appropriate*

[12]*rusted or corroded*

[13]*fight*

[14]*drove*

Which then most sought where most might not be found,
Being one too many by my weary self—
125   Pursu'd my humour, not pursuing his,
And gladly shunn'd who gladly fled from me.
MON: Many a morning hath he there been seen,
With tears augmenting the fresh morning's dew,
Adding to clouds more clouds with his deep sighs;
130   But all so soon as the all-cheering sun
Should in the farthest East begin to draw
The shady curtains from Aurora's[15] bed,

15*goddess of the dawn*

Away from light steals home my heavy son
And private in his chamber pens himself,
135   Shuts up his windows, locks fair daylight out
And makes himself an artificial night.
Black and portentous must this humour prove
Unless good counsel may the cause remove.
BEN: My noble uncle, do you know the cause?
140 MON: I neither know it nor can learn of him.
BEN: Have you importun'd[16] him by any means?

16*question*

MON: Both by myself and many other friends;
But he, his own affections' counsellor,
Is to himself—I will not say how true—
145   But to himself so secret and so close,
So far from sounding[17] and discovery,

17*probing*

As is the bud bit with an envious worm
Ere[18] he can spread his sweet leaves to the air

18*before*

Or dedicate his beauty to the sun.
150   Could we but learn from whence his sorrows grow,
We would as willingly give cure as know.

Enter Romeo.

BEN: See, where he comes. So please you, step aside,
I'll know his grievance, or be much denied.
MON: I would thou wert so happy by thy stay
155   To hear true shrift.[19] Come, madam, let's away,

19*confession*

Exeunt Montague and Wife.

BEN: Good morrow, cousin.

ROM: Is the day so young?

BEN: But new[20] struck nine.

[20]*just now*

ROM: Ay me! sad hours seem long.

160   Was that my father that went hence so fast?

BEN: It was. What sadness lengthens Romeo's hours?

ROM: Not having that, which, having, makes them short.

BEN: In love?

ROM: Out—

165 BEN: Of love?

ROM: Out of her favour, where I am in love.

BEN: Alas that love, so gentle in his view,
     Should be so tyrannous and rough in proof!

ROM: Alas that love, whose view is muffled[21] still,

[21]*blocked*
    [because Cupid,
    the god of love,
    was traditional-
    ly shown wear-
    ing a blindfold]

170   Should without eyes see pathways to his will!
     Where shall we dine? O me! What fray was here?
     Yet tell me not, for I have heard it all.
     Here's much to do with hate, but more with love.
     Why then, O brawling love! O loving hate!

175   O any thing, of nothing first create!
     O heavy lightness! serious vanity!
     Misshapen chaos of well-seeming forms!
     Feather of lead, bright smoke, cold fire, sick health!
     Still-waking sleep, that is not what it is!

180   This love feel I, that feel no love in this.
     Dost thou not laugh?

BEN: No, coz,[22] I rather weep.

[22]*cousin*

ROM: Good heart, at what?

BEN: At thy good heart's oppression.

185 ROM: Why, such is love's transgression.
     Griefs of mine own lie heavy in my breast,
     Which thou wilt propagate, to have it prest
     With more of thine. This love that thou hast shown
     Doth add more grief to too much of mine own.

190   Love is a smoke rais'd with the fume of sighs;
     Being purg'd, a fire sparkling in lovers' eyes;
     Being vex'd, a sea nourish'd with lovers' tears.
     What is it else? A madness most discreet,
     A choking gall, and a preserving sweet.

195   Farewell, my coz.

BEN: Soft! I will go along.
       An if you leave me so, you do me wrong.
ROM: Tut! I have lost myself; I am not here:
       This is not Romeo, he's some otherwhere.
200 BEN: Tell me in sadness, who is that you love?
ROM: What, shall I groan and tell thee?
BEN: Groan? Why, no;
       But sadly tell me who.
ROM: Bid a sick man in sadness make his will.
205   Ah, word ill urg'd to one that is so ill!
       In sadness, cousin, I do love a woman.
BEN: I aim'd so near when I suppos'd you lov'd.
ROM: A right good markman! And she's fair I love.
BEN: A right fair mark, fair coz, is soonest hit.
210 ROM: Well, in that hit you miss. She'll not be hit
       With Cupid's arrow. She hath Dian's[23] wit,
       And, in strong proof of chastity well arm'd,
       From Love's weak childish bow she lives unharm'd.
       She will not stay[24] the siege of loving terms,
215   Nor bide th' encounter of assailing eyes,
       Nor ope her lap to saint-seducing gold.
       O, she's rich in beauty; only poor
       That, when she dies, with beauty dies her store.
BEN: Then she hath sworn that she will still live chaste?
220 ROM: She hath, and in that sparing makes huge waste;
       For beauty, starv'd with her severity,
       Cuts beauty off from all posterity.[25]
       She is too fair, too wise, wisely too fair,
       To merit bliss by making me despair.
225   She hath forsworn to love, and in that vow
       Do I live dead that live to tell it now.
BEN: Be rul'd by me: forget to think of her.
ROM: O, teach me how I should forget to think!
BEN: By giving liberty unto thine eyes.
230   Examine other beauties.
ROM: 'Tis the way
       To call hers, exquisite, in question more.
       These happy masks that kiss fair ladies' brows,
       Being black puts us in mind they hide the fair.
235   He that is strucken blind cannot forget

[23]*goddess of the hunt and female chastity*

[24]*endure*

[25]*i.e., a chaste beauty has no children*

The precious treasure of his eyesight lost.
Show me a mistress that is passing fair,
What doth her beauty serve but as a note
Where I may read who pass'd that passing fair?
240   Farewell. Thou canst not teach me to forget.
BEN: I'll pay that doctrine, or else die in debt.

Exeunt.

SCENE II
A Street.

Enter Capulet, Paris, and Servant.

CAP: But Montague is bound as well as I,
In penalty alike; and 'tis not hard, I think,
For men so old as we to keep the peace.
PAR: Of honourable reckoning are you both,
5   And pity 'tis you liv'd at odds so long.
But now, my lord, what say you to my suit?
CAP: But saying o'er what I have said before:
My child is yet a stranger in the world,
She hath not seen the change of fourteen years;
10   Let two more summers wither in their pride
Ere we may think her ripe to be a bride.
PAR: Younger than she are happy mothers made.
CAP: And too soon marr'd are those so early made.
The earth hath swallowed all my hopes but she;[26]
15   She is the hopeful lady of my earth.
But woo her, gentle Paris, get her heart;
My will to her consent is but a part.
An[27] she agree, within her scope of choice
Lies my consent and fair according voice.
20   This night I hold an old accustom'd feast,
Whereto I have invited many a guest,
Such as I love; and you among the store,
One more, most welcome, makes my number more.
At my poor house look to behold this night

[26] *[Juliet is the Capulets' only surviving child.]*

[27] *If*

25   Earth-treading stars that make dark heaven light.
      Such comfort as do lusty young men feel
      When well-apparell'd April on the heel
      Of limping Winter treads, even such delight
      Among fresh female buds shall you this night
30   Inherit[28] at my house. Hear all, all see,
      And like her most whose merit most shall be;
      Which, amongst view of many, mine, being one,
      May stand in number, though in reck'ning none.[29]
      Come, go with me.   *To Servant, giving him a paper*
35   Go, sirrah, trudge about
      Through fair Verona; find those persons out
      Whose names are written there, and to them say,
      My house and welcome on their pleasure stay.—

                    Exeunt Capulet and Paris.

      SERV: Find them out whose names are written here?
40   It is written that the shoemaker should meddle with his
      yard and the tailor with his last, the fisher with his
      pencil, and the painter with his nets; but I am sent to
      find those persons whose names are here writ, and can
      never find what names the writing person hath here
45   writ.[30] I must to the learned. In good time!

Enter Benvolio and Romeo.

      BEN: Tut, man! one fire burns out another's burning;
            One pain is lessened by another's anguish;
            Turn giddy, and be holp by backward turning;
            One desperate grief cures with another's languish.
50   Take thou some new infection to thy eye,
            And the rank poison of the old will die.
      ROM: Your plantain leaf[31] is excellent for that.
      BEN: For what, I pray thee?
      ROM: For your broken shin.
55   BEN: Why, Romeo, art thou mad?
      ROM: Not mad, but bound more than a madman is;
            Shut up in Prison, kept without my food,
            Whipp'd and tormented and–   *Spoken to servant*
                  God-eve, good fellow.

[28]*to enjoy, to possess*

[29]*i.e., my daughter will be one of the people there, but you may not count her among the ones you like most.*

[30]*[the servant cannot read]*

[31]*a medicinal plant*

SERV: *To Romeo*   I pray, sir, can you read?

60 ROM: Ay, mine own fortune in my misery.

SERV: Perhaps you have learned it without book. But I pray, can you read any thing you see?

ROM: Ay, If I know the letters and the language.

SERV: Ye say honestly.[32] Rest you merry!

65 ROM: Stay, fellow; I can read.   *He reads.*

'Signior Martino and his wife and daughters;

County Anselme and his beauteous sisters;

The lady widow of Vitruvio;

Signior Placentio and his lovely nieces;

70 Mercutio and his brother Valentine;

Mine uncle Capulet, his wife, and daughters;

My fair niece Rosaline and Livia;

Signior Valentio and his cousin Tybalt;

Lucio and the lively Helena.'

Gives back the paper.

75 A fair assembly. Whither should they come?

SERV: Up.

ROM: Whither to supper?

SERV: To our house.

ROM: Whose house?

80 SERV: My master's.

ROM: Indeed, I should have ask'd you that before.

SERV: Now I'll tell you without asking. My master is the great rich Capulet; and if you be not of the house of Montagues, I pray, come and crush a cup of wine. Rest

85 you merry!   *Exit.*

BEN: At this same ancient feast of Capulet's

Sups the fair Rosaline whom thou so lov'st;

With all the admired beauties of Verona.

Go thither, and with unattainted[33] eye

90 Compare her face with some that I shall show,

And I will make thee think thy swan a crow.

ROM: When the devout religion of mine eye[34]

Maintains such falsehood, then turn tears to fires.

And these, who often drown'd, could never die,

95 Transparent heretics, be burnt for liars!

One fairer than my love? The all-seeing sun

Ne'er saw her match since first the world begun.

---

[32] [The servant interprets this as meaning Romeo cannot read]

[33] unprejudiced

[34] [Religious heretics were often burnt at the stake; Romeo says that his tears would be like such heretics (i.e., false) if he loved a woman besides Rosaline]

BEN: Tut! you saw her fair, none else being by,
     Herself pois'd with herself in either eye;
100   But in that crystal scales let there be weigh'd
     Your lady's love against some other maid
     That I will show you shining at this feast,
     And she shall scant show well that now seems best.
105 ROM: I'll go along, no such sight to be shown,
     But to rejoice in splendour of my own.

                                        Exeunt.

SCENE III
Capulet's House.

Enter Lady Capulet, and Nurse.

LADY CAP: Nurse, where's my daughter? Call her forth to me.
NURSE: Now, by my maidenhead at twelve year old, I bade
     her come. What, lamb! what ladybird!35 God forbid!
     Where's this girl? What, Juliet!

Enter Juliet.

  5 JUL: How now? Who calls?
NURSE: Your mother.
JUL: Madam, I am here.
     What is your will?
LADY CAP: This is the matter—Nurse, give leave awhile,
10   We must talk in secret. Nurse, come back again;
     I have remember'd me, thou shalt hear our counsel.
     Thou knowest my daughter's of a pretty age.
NURSE: Faith, I can tell her age unto an hour.
LADY CAP: She's not fourteen.
15 NURSE: I'll lay fourteen of my teeth—
     And yet, to my teen36 be it spoken, I have but four—
     She is not fourteen. How long is it now
     To Lammastide?
LADY CAP: A fortnight and odd days.
20 NURSE: Even or odd, of all days in the year,

35*term of endear-
ment; also, a
female of loose
morals*

36*sorrow*

Come Lammas Eve at night shall she be fourteen.
Susan and she (God rest all Christian souls!)
Were of an age. Well, Susan is with God;
She was too good for me. But, as I said,

25   On Lammas Eve at night shall she be fourteen;
That shall she, marry; I remember it well.
'Tis since the earthquake now eleven years;
And she was wean'd (I never shall forget it),
Of all the days of the year, upon that day;

30   For I had then laid wormwood[37] to my dug,
Sitting in the sun under the dovehouse wall.
My lord and you were then at Mantua.
Nay, I do bear a brain. But, as I said,
When it[38] did taste the wormwood on the nipple

35   Of my dug and felt it bitter, pretty fool,
To see it tetchy and fall out with the dug!
Shake, quoth the dovehouse! 'Twas no need, I trow,
To bid me trudge.
And since that time it is eleven years,

40   For then she could stand high-lone; nay, by th' rood,[39]
She could have run and waddled all about;
 For even the day before, she broke her brow;
And then my husband (God be with his soul!
A' was a merry man) took up the child.

45   'Yea,' quoth he, 'dost thou fall upon thy face?
Thou wilt fall backward when thou hast more wit;
Wilt thou not, Jule?' and, by my holidame,
The pretty wretch left crying, and said 'Ay.'
To see now how a jest shall come about!

50   I warrant, an I should live a thousand years,
I never should forget it. 'Wilt thou not, Jule?' quoth he,
And, pretty fool, it stinted,[40] and said 'Ay.'
LADY CAP: Enough of this. I pray thee hold thy peace.
NURSE: Yes, madam. Yet I cannot choose but laugh

55   To think it should leave crying and say 'Ay.'
And yet, I warrant, it had upon it brow
A bump as big as a young cock'rel's stone;
A perilous knock; and it cried bitterly.
Yea,' quoth my husband, 'fall'st upon thy face?

60   Thou wilt fall backward when thou comest to age;

[37] a bitter juice used to wean a child

[38] Juliet

[39] cross

[40] stopped crying

Wilt thou not, Jule?' It stinted, and said 'Ay.'
JUL: And stint thou too, I pray thee, nurse, say I.
NURSE: Peace, I have done. God mark thee to his grace!
    Thou wast the prettiest babe that e'er I nurs'd.
65   An I might live to see thee married once,
    I have my wish.
LADY CAP: Marry, that 'marry' is the very theme
    I came to talk of. Tell me, daughter Juliet,
    How stands your disposition to be married?
70 JUL: It is an honour that I dream not of.
NURSE: An honour? Were not I thine only nurse,
    I would say thou hadst suck'd wisdom from thy teat.
LADY CAP: Well, think of marriage now. Younger than you,
    Here in Verona, ladies of esteem,
75   Are made already mothers. By my count,
    I was your mother much upon these years
    That you are now a maid. Thus then in brief:
    The valiant Paris seeks you for his love.
NURSE: A man, young lady! lady, such a man
80   As all the world- why he's a man of wax.[41]
LADY CAP: Verona's summer hath not such a flower.
NURSE: Nay, he's a flower, in faith—a very flower.
LADY CAP: What say you? Can you love the gentleman?
    This night you shall behold him at our feast.
85   Read o'er the volume of young Paris' face,
    And find delight writ there with beauty's pen;
    Examine every married lineament,
    And see how one another lends content;
    And what obscur'd in this fair volume lies
90   Find written in the margent of his eyes,
    This precious book of love, this unbound lover,
    To beautify him only lacks a cover.
    The fish lives in the sea, and 'tis much pride
    For fair without the fair within to hide.
95   That book in many's eyes doth share the glory,
    That in gold clasps locks in the golden story;
    So shall you share all that he doth possess,
    By having him making yourself no less.
NURSE: No less? Nay, bigger! Women grow by men.
100 LADY CAP: Speak briefly, can you like of Paris' love?

[41] *a handsome man*

42*let fly and*
pierce like an
arrow

JUL: I'll look to like, if looking liking move;
But no more deep will I endart[42] mine eye
Than your consent gives strength to make it fly.

Enter Servingman.

SERV: Madam, the guests are come, supper serv'd up, you
105   call'd, my young lady ask'd for, the nurse curs'd in the
pantry, and everything in extremity. I must hence to
wait. I beseech you follow straight.
LADY CAP: We follow thee.   *Exit Servingman.*
Juliet, the County stays.
110 NURSE: Go, girl, seek happy nights to happy days.
Exeunt.

SCENE IV
A street.

Enter Romeo, Mercutio, Benvolio, with five or six other
Maskers; Torchbearers.

ROM: What, shall this speech be spoke for our excuse?
Or shall we on without apology?
BEN: The date is out of such prolixity.[43]

43*such wordiness*
is outdated
[It used to be the
custom that
guests who
wished to attend
incognito and
wore a mask sent
a messenger
before them to
apologize to the
host.]

44*dance*

45*heavy-hearted*

5   We'll have no Cupid hoodwink'd with a scarf,
Bearing a Tartar's painted bow of lath,
Scaring the ladies like a crowkeeper;
Nor no without-book prologue, faintly spoke
After the prompter, for our entrance;
10   But, let them measure us by what they will,
We'll measure them a measure,[44] and be gone.
ROM: Give me a torch. I am not for this ambling.
Being but heavy,[45] I will bear the light.
MER: Nay, gentle Romeo, we must have you dance.
15 ROM: Not I, believe me. You have dancing shoes
With nimble soles; I have a soul of lead
So stakes me to the ground I cannot move.
MER: You are a lover. Borrow Cupid's wings

And soar with them above a common bound.

20 ROM: I am too sore enpiercèd with his shaft
To soar with his light feathers; and so bound
I cannot bound a pitch above dull woe.
Under love's heavy burden do I sink.

MER: And, to sink in it, should you burden love—
25 Too great oppression for a tender thing.

ROM: Is love a tender thing? It is too rough,
Too rude, too boist'rous, and it pricks like thorn.

MER: If love be rough with you, be rough with love.
Prick love for pricking, and you beat love down.
30 Give me a case to put my visage[46] in.
A visor for a visor![47] What care I
What curious eye doth quote deformities?
Here are the beetle brows shall blush for me.

BEN: Come, knock and enter; and no sooner in
35 But every man betake him to his legs.

ROM: A torch for me! Let wantons light of heart
Tickle the senseless rushes[48] with their heels;
For I am proverb'd with a grandsire phrase,
I'll be a candle-holder and look on;
40 The game was ne'er so fair, and I am done.

MER: Tut! dun's the mouse,[49] the constable's own word!
If thou art dun, we'll draw thee from the mire[50]
Or (save your reverence) love, wherein thou stick'st
Up to the ears. Come, we burn daylight, ho!

45 ROM: Nay, that's not so.

MER: I mean, sir, in delay
We waste our lights in vain, like lamps by day.
Take our good meaning, for our judgment sits
Five times in that ere once in our five wits.

50 ROM: And we mean well, in going to this mask;
But 'tis no wit to go.

MER: Why, may one ask?

ROM: I dreamt a dream to-night.

MER: And so did I.

55 ROM: Well, what was yours?

MER: That dreamers often lie.

ROM: In bed asleep, while they do dream things true.

MER: O, then I see Queen Mab[51] hath been with you.

[46]mask

[47]a mask to cover a mask

[48]dry grasses spread on the dance floor

[49]be quiet

[50] "Dun" means "dark and gloomy," which describes Romeo's mood. "Dun" is also the name of a horse in a game called "drawing dun out of the mire."

[51]queen of the fairies; Mercutio's description of her reveals his wild imagination

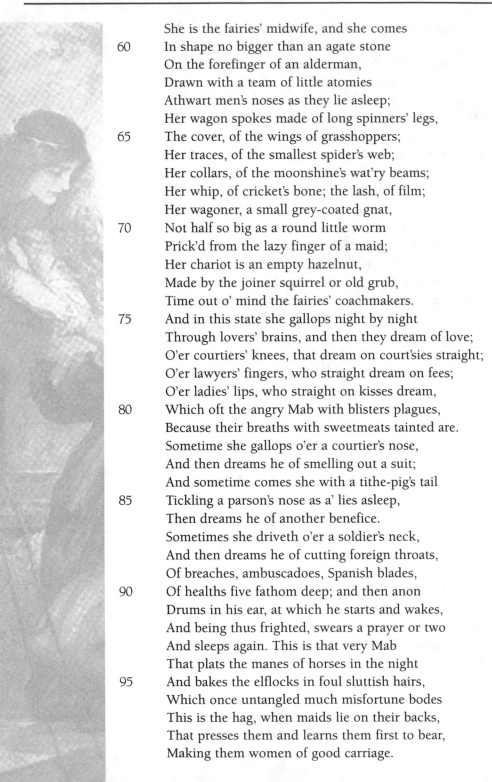

She is the fairies' midwife, and she comes
60   In shape no bigger than an agate stone
On the forefinger of an alderman,
Drawn with a team of little atomies
Athwart men's noses as they lie asleep;
Her wagon spokes made of long spinners' legs,
65   The cover, of the wings of grasshoppers;
Her traces, of the smallest spider's web;
Her collars, of the moonshine's wat'ry beams;
Her whip, of cricket's bone; the lash, of film;
Her wagoner, a small grey-coated gnat,
70   Not half so big as a round little worm
Prick'd from the lazy finger of a maid;
Her chariot is an empty hazelnut,
Made by the joiner squirrel or old grub,
Time out o' mind the fairies' coachmakers.
75   And in this state she gallops night by night
Through lovers' brains, and then they dream of love;
O'er courtiers' knees, that dream on court'sies straight;
O'er lawyers' fingers, who straight dream on fees;
O'er ladies' lips, who straight on kisses dream,
80   Which oft the angry Mab with blisters plagues,
Because their breaths with sweetmeats tainted are.
Sometime she gallops o'er a courtier's nose,
And then dreams he of smelling out a suit;
And sometime comes she with a tithe-pig's tail
85   Tickling a parson's nose as a' lies asleep,
Then dreams he of another benefice.
Sometimes she driveth o'er a soldier's neck,
And then dreams he of cutting foreign throats,
Of breaches, ambuscadoes, Spanish blades,
90   Of healths five fathom deep; and then anon
Drums in his ear, at which he starts and wakes,
And being thus frighted, swears a prayer or two
And sleeps again. This is that very Mab
That plats the manes of horses in the night
95   And bakes the elflocks in foul sluttish hairs,
Which once untangled much misfortune bodes
This is the hag, when maids lie on their backs,
That presses them and learns them first to bear,
Making them women of good carriage.

100   This is she—
      ROM: Peace, peace, Mercutio, peace!
        Thou talk'st of nothing.
      MER: True, I talk of dreams;
        Which are the children of an idle brain,
105   Begot of nothing but vain fantasy;
        Which is as thin of substance as the air,
        And more inconstant than the wind, who wooes
        Even now the frozen bosom of the north
        And, being anger'd, puffs away from thence,
110   Turning his face to the dew-dropping south.
      BEN: This wind you talk of blows us from ourselves.
        Supper is done, and we shall come too late.
      ROM: I fear, too early; for my mind misgives
        Some consequence, yet hanging in the stars,
115   Shall bitterly begin his fearful date
        With this night's revels and expire the term
        Of a despised life, clos'd in my breast,
        By some vile forfeit of untimely death.
        But He, that hath the steerage of my course,
120   Direct my sail! On, lusty gentlemen!
      BEN: Strike, drum.

They march about the stage. Exeunt.

SCENE V
Capulet's House.

Servingmen come forth with napkins.

      1. SERV: Where's Potpan, that he helps not to take away?
        He shift a trencher! he scrape a trencher![52]
      2. SERV: When good manners shall lie all in one or two
5   men's hands, and they unwash'd too, 'tis a foul thing.
      1. SERV: Away with the joint-stools, remove the court-cup-
        board, look to the plate. Good thou, save me a piece of
        marchpane[53] and, as thou lovest me, let the porter let in
        Susan Grindstone and Nell. Anthony, and Potpan!

[52]*a serving dish*

[53]*almond cake*

2. SERV: Ay, boy, ready.
Enter Third and Fourth servants.

10

1. SERV: You are look'd for and call'd for, ask'd for and
sought for, in the great chamber.
3. SERV: We cannot be here and there too. Cheerly, boys!
Be brisk awhile, and the longer liver take all. *Exeunt.*

*Enter the Maskers, Enter, (with Servants) Capulet, his Wife,
Juliet, Tybalt, and all the Guests and Gentlewomen to the
Maskers.*

15 **CAP:** Welcome, gentlemen! Ladies that have their toes
Unplagu'd with corns will have a bout with you.
Ah ha, my mistresses! which of you all
Will now deny to dance? She that makes dainty,
She, I'll swear, hath corns. Am I come near ye now?
20   Welcome, gentlemen! I have seen the day
That I have worn a visor and could tell
A whispering tale in a fair lady's ear,
Such as would please. 'Tis gone, 'tis gone, 'tis gone!
You are welcome, gentlemen! Come, musicians, play.
A hall, a hall! give room! and foot it, girls.
25 *Music plays, and they dance.*
More light, you knaves! and turn the tables up,
And quench the fire, the room is grown too hot.
Ah, sirrah, this unlook'd-for sport comes well.
Nay, sit, nay, sit, good cousin Capulet,
30   For you and I are past our dancing days.
How long is't now since last yourself and I
Were in a mask?
2. CAP: By'r Lady,[54] thirty years.
CAP: What, man? 'Tis not so much, 'tis not so much!
35   'Tis since the nuptial of Lucentio,
Come Pentecost as quickly as it will,
Some five-and-twenty years, and then we mask'd.
2. CAP: 'Tis more, 'tis more! His son is elder, sir;
His son is thirty.
40 **CAP:** Will you tell me that?
His son was but a ward two years ago.

[54] *by Our Lady
(the Virgin
Mary)*

ROM: *To a Servingman.*   What lady's that, which doth enrich the hand
    Of yonder knight?
45 SERV: I know not, sir.
ROM: O, she doth teach the torches to burn bright!
    It seems she hangs upon the cheek of night
    Like a rich jewel in an Ethiop's ear—
    Beauty too rich for use, for earth too dear!
50   So shows a snowy dove trooping with crows
    As yonder lady o'er her fellows shows.
    The measure done, I'll watch her place of stand
    And, touching hers, make blessed my rude hand.
    Did my heart love till now? Forswear it, sight!
55   For I ne'er saw true beauty till this night.
TYB: This, by his voice, should be a Montague.
    Fetch me my rapier, boy. What, dares the slave
    Come hither, cover'd with an antic[55] face,
    To fleer and scorn at our solemnity?
60   Now, by the stock and honour of my kin,
    To strike him dead I hold it not a sin.
CAP: Why, how now, kinsman? Wherefore storm you so?
TYB: Uncle, this is a Montague, our foe;
    A villain, that is hither come in spite
65   To scorn at our solemnity this night.
CAP: Young Romeo is it?
TYB: 'Tis he, that villain Romeo.
CAP: Content thee, gentle coz, let him alone.
    He bears him like a portly gentleman,
70   And, to say truth, Verona brags of him
    To be a virtuous and well-govern'd youth.
    I would not for the wealth of all this town
    Here in my house do him disparagement.
    Therefore be patient, take no note of him.
75   It is my will; the which if thou respect,
    Show a fair presence and put off these frowns,
    An ill-beseeming semblance for a feast.
TYB: It fits when such a villain is a guest.
    I'll not endure him.
80 CAP: He shall be endur'd.
    What, goodman boy? I say he shall. Go to!

[55] *comic (referring to Romeo's mask)*

Am I the master here, or you? Go to!
You'll not endure him? God shall mend my soul!
You'll make a mutiny among my guests!

85   You will set cock-a-hoop![56] you'll be the man!

TYB: Why, uncle, 'tis a shame.

CAP: Go to, go to!
You are a saucy boy. Is't so, indeed?
This trick may chance to scathe[57] you. I know what.

90   You must contrary me! Marry, 'tis time—
Well said, my hearts!—You are a princox[58]—go!
Be quiet, or—More light, more light!—For shame!
I'll make you quiet; what!—Cheerly, my hearts!

TYB: Patience perforce with wilful choler meeting

95   Makes my flesh tremble in their different greeting.
I will withdraw; but this intrusion shall,
Now seeming sweet, convert to bitt'rest gall.   *Exit.*

ROM: If I profane[59] with my unworthiest hand
This holy shrine,[60] the gentle fine is this:

100   My lips, two blushing pilgrims, ready stand
To smooth that rough touch with a tender kiss.

JUL: Good pilgrim, you do wrong your hand too much,
Which mannerly devotion shows in this;
For saints have hands that pilgrims' hands do touch,

105   And palm to palm is holy palmers' kiss.

ROM: Have not saints lips, and holy palmers too?

JUL: Ay, pilgrim, lips that they must use in prayer.

ROM: O, then, dear saint, let lips do what hands do!
They pray; grant thou, lest faith turn to despair.

110 JUL: Saints do not move, though grant for prayers' sake.

ROM: Then move not while my prayer's effect I take.
Thus from my lips, by thine my sin is purg'd.

Kisses her.

JUL: Then have my lips the sin that they have took.

ROM: Sin from my lips? O trespass sweetly urg'd!

115   Give me my sin again.   *Kisses her.*

JUL: You kiss by th' book.[61]

NURSE: Madam, your mother craves a word with you.

ROM: What is her mother?

NURSE: Marry, bachelor,

120   Her mother is the lady of the house.

---

[56] start a fight

[57] harm

[58] strutting rooster

[59] pollute

[60] [Romeo compares Juliet to a holy shrine and offers his lips as pilgrims to kiss her. She responds that palmers (another word for pilgrim) kiss hand to hand (palm to palm).]

[61] properly

And a good lady, and a wise and virtuous.
I nurs'd her daughter that you talk'd withal.
I tell you, he that can lay hold of her
Shall have the chinks.[62]   [62]*money*

125 ROM: Is she a Capulet?
O dear account! my life is my foe's debt.
BEN: Away, be gone; the sport is at the best.[63]   [63]*the best part is past*
ROM: Ay, so I fear; the more is my unrest.
CAP: Nay, gentlemen, prepare not to be gone;
130   We have a trifling foolish banquet towards.
Is it e'en so? Why then, I thank you all.
I thank you, honest gentlemen. Good night.
More torches here!   *Exeunt Maskers.*
Come on then, let's to bed.
135   Ah, sirrah, by my fay,[64] it waxes late;   [63]*faith*
I'll to my rest.

Exeunt all but Juliet and Nurse.

JUL: Come hither, Nurse. What is yon gentleman?
NURSE: The son and heir of old Tiberio.
JUL: What's he that now is going out of door?
140 NURSE: Marry, that, I think, be young Petruchio.
JUL: What's he that follows there, that would not dance?
NURSE: I know not.
JUL: Go ask his name.—If he be married,
My grave is like to be my wedding bed.
145 NURSE: His name is Romeo, and a Montague,
The only son of your great enemy.
JUL: My only love, sprung from my only hate!
Too early seen unknown, and known too late!
Prodigious birth of love it is to me
150   That I must love a loathed enemy.
NURSE: What's this? what's this?
JUL: A rhyme I learn'd even now
Of one I danc'd withal.
                        One calls within 'Juliet.'
NURSE: Anon, anon!
155   Come, let's away; the strangers all are gone.   *Exeunt.*

ACT II

PROLOGUE

Enter Chorus.

CHOR: Now old desire doth in his deathbed lie,
    And young affection gapes to be his heir;
    That fair for which love groan'd for and would die,
    With tender Juliet match'd, is now not fair.
5   Now Romeo is belov'd, and loves again,
    Alike bewitched by the charm of looks;
    But to his foe suppos'd he must complain,
    And she steal love's sweet bait from fearful hooks.
    Being held a foe, he may not have access
10   To breathe such vows as lovers use to swear,
    And she as much in love, her means much less
    To meet her new beloved anywhere;
    But passion lends them power, time means, to meet,
    Temp'ring extremities with extreme sweet.

                             Exit.

SCENE I

A lane by the wall of Capulet's orchard.

Enter Romeo alone.

ROM: Can I go forward when my heart is here?
      Turn back, dull earth, and find thy centre[1] out.

Climbs the wall and leaps down within it.
Enter Benvolio with Mercutio.

BEN: Romeo! my cousin Romeo! Romeo!
MER: He is wise,
5   And, on my life, hath stol'n him home to bed.
BEN: He ran this way, and leapt this orchard wall.
      Call, good Mercutio.
MER: Nay, I'll conjure[2] too.
      Romeo! humours! madman! passion! lover!
10   Appear thou in the likeness of a sigh;
      Speak but one rhyme, and I am satisfied!
      Cry but 'Ay me!' pronounce but 'love' and 'dove';
      Speak to my gossip Venus one fair word,
      One nickname for her purblind son[3] and heir,
15   Young Adam Cupid, he that shot so trim
      When King Cophetua[4] lov'd the beggar maid!
      He heareth not, he stirreth not, be moveth not;
      The ape is dead, and I must conjure him.
      I conjure thee by Rosaline's bright eyes.
20   By her high forehead and her scarlet lip,
      By her fine foot, straight leg, and quivering thigh,
      And the demesnes[5] that there adjacent lie,
      That in thy likeness thou appear to us!
BEN: An if he hear thee, thou wilt anger him.
25 MER: This cannot anger him. 'Twould anger him
      To raise a spirit in his mistress' circle
      Of some strange nature, letting it there stand
      Till she had laid it and conjur'd it down.
      That were some spite; my invocation
30   Is fair and honest: in his mistress' name,
      I conjure only but to raise up him.

[1] *i.e., Juliet*

[2] *use spells*

[3] *Cupid, often pictured as blindfolded*

[4] *African king who fell in love with a servant*

[5] *regions*

BEN: Come, he hath hid himself among these trees
     To be consorted with the humorous night.
     Blind is his love and best befits the dark.
35 MER: If love be blind, love cannot hit the mark.
     Now will he sit under a medlar tree
     And wish his mistress were that kind of fruit
     As maids call medlars[6] when they laugh alone.
     O, Romeo, that she were, O that she were
40   An open et cetera,[7] thou a pop'rin pear!
     Romeo, good night. I'll to my truckle-bed;
     This field-bed is too cold for me to sleep.
     Come, shall we go?
   BEN: Go then, for 'tis in vain
45   'To seek him here that means not to be found.

                               Exeunt.

[6] *an apple-like fruit of unusual shape*

[7] *[he won't say the actual word]*

SCENE II
Capulet's orchard.

Enter Romeo.

ROM: He[8] jests at scars that never felt a wound.
Enter Juliet above at a window.
     But soft! What light through yonder window breaks?
     It is the East, and Juliet is the sun!
     Arise, fair sun, and kill the envious moon,
5   Who is already sick and pale with grief
     That thou her maid art far more fair than she.[9]
     Be not her maid, since she is envious.
     Her vestal livery is but sick and green,
     And none but fools do wear it. Cast it off.
10   It is my lady; O, it is my love!
     O that she knew she were!
     She speaks, yet she says nothing. What of that?
     Her eye discourses; I will answer it.
     I am too bold; 'tis not to me she speaks.
15   Two of the fairest stars in all the heaven,
     Having some business, do entreat her eyes

[8] *Mercutio [Romeo has overheard Mercutio's joke from the previous scene.]*

[9] *Juliet (the sun) is more beautiful than the moon.*

To twinkle in their spheres till they return.
What if her eyes were there, they in her head?
The brightness of her cheek would shame those stars
20 As daylight doth a lamp; her eyes in heaven
Would through the airy region stream so bright
That birds would sing and think it were not night.
See how she leans her cheek upon her hand!
O that I were a glove upon that hand,
25 That I might touch that cheek!

JUL: Ay me!

ROM: She speaks.

O, speak again, bright angel! for thou art
As glorious to this night, being o'er my head,
30 As is a winged messenger of heaven
Unto the white-upturned wond'ring eyes
Of mortals that fall back to gaze on him
When he bestrides the lazy-pacing clouds
And sails upon the bosom of the air.

[10]*why*

35 JUL: O Romeo, Romeo! wherefore[10] art thou Romeo?
Deny thy father and refuse thy name!
Or, if thou wilt not, be but sworn my love,
And I'll no longer be a Capulet.

ROM: *Aside.*   Shall I hear more, or shall I speak at this?

40 JUL: 'Tis but thy name that is my enemy.
Thou art thyself, though not a Montague.
What's Montague? it is nor hand, nor foot,
Nor arm, nor face, nor any other part
Belonging to a man. O, be some other name!
45 What's in a name? That which we call a rose
By any other name would smell as sweet.
So Romeo would, were he not Romeo call'd,
Retain that dear perfection which he owes
Without that title. Romeo, doff thy name;
50 And for that name, which is no part of thee,
Take all myself.

ROM: I take thee at thy word.

Call me but love, and I'll be new baptiz'd;
Henceforth I never will be Romeo.

[11]*hidden*

55 JUL: What man art thou that, thus bescreen'd[11] in night,
So stumblest on my counsel?

ROM:　By a name
　　　I know not how to tell thee who I am.
　　　My name, dear saint, is hateful to myself,
60　　Because it is an enemy to thee.
　　　Had I it written, I would tear the word.
JUL:　My ears have yet not drunk a hundred words
　　　Of that tongue's utterance, yet I know the sound.
　　　Art thou not Romeo, and a Montague?
65　ROM:　Neither, fair maid, if either thee dislike.
JUL:　How cam'st thou hither, tell me, and wherefore?
　　　The orchard walls are high and hard to climb,
　　　And the place death, considering who thou art,
　　　If any of my kinsmen find thee here.
70　ROM:　With love's light wings did I o'erperch these walls;
　　　For stony limits cannot hold love out,
　　　And what love can do, that dares love attempt.
　　　Therefore thy kinsmen are no stop to me.
JUL:　If they do see thee, they will murder thee.
75　ROM:　Alack, there lies more peril in thine eye
　　　Than twenty of their swords! Look thou but sweet,
　　　And I am proof[12] against their enmity.
JUL:　I would not for the world they saw thee here.
ROM:　I have night's cloak to hide me from their eyes;
80　　And but thou love me, let them find me here.
　　　My life were better ended by their hate
　　　Than death prorogued,[13] wanting of thy love.
JUL:　By whose direction found'st thou out this place?
ROM:　By love, that first did prompt me to inquire.
85　　He lent me counsel, and I lent him eyes.
　　　I am no pilot; yet, wert thou as far
　　　As that vast shore wash'd with the farthest sea,
　　　I would adventure[14] for such merchandise.
JUL:　Thou knowest the mask of night is on my face;
90　　Else would a maiden blush bepaint my cheek
　　　For that which thou hast heard me speak to-night.
　　　Fain[15] would I dwell on form,[16] fain, fain deny
　　　What I have spoke; but farewell complement![17]
　　　Dost thou love me? I know thou wilt say 'Ay';
95　　And I will take thy word. Yet, if thou swear'st,
　　　Thou mayst prove false. At lovers' perjuries,

[12]*protected*

[13]*drawn out, pro-longed*

[14]*travel, venture*

[15]*gladly*

[16]*formality, politness*

[17]*etiquette*

[18]*king of the gods*

          They say Jove[18] laughs. O gentle Romeo,
          If thou dost love, pronounce it faithfully.
          Or if thou thinkest I am too quickly won,
100   I'll frown, and be perverse, and say thee nay,
          So thou wilt woo; but else, not for the world.

[19]*foolish*

          In truth, fair Montague, I am too fond,[19]

[20]*silly*

          And therefore thou mayst think my haviour light;[20]
          But trust me, gentleman, I'll prove more true

[21]*cleverness*

105   Than those that have more cunning[21] to be strange.
          I should have been more strange, I must confess,
          But that thou overheard'st, ere I was ware,
          My true love's passion. Therefore pardon me,
          And not impute this yielding to light love,
110   Which the dark night hath so discovered.
    ROM: Lady, by yonder blessed moon I swear,
          That tips with silver all these fruit-tree tops—
    JUL: O, swear not by the moon, the inconstant moon,
          That monthly changes in her circled orb,
115   Lest that thy love prove likewise variable.
    ROM: What shall I swear by?
    JUL: Do not swear at all;
          Or if thou wilt, swear by thy gracious self,
          Which is the god of my idolatry,
120   And I'll believe thee.
    ROM: If my heart's dear love—
    JUL: Well, do not swear. Although I joy in thee,
          I have no joy of this contract to-night.
          It is too rash, too unadvis'd, too sudden;
125   Too like the lightning, which doth cease to be
          Ere one can say 'It lightens.' Sweet, good night!
          This bud of love, by summer's ripening breath,
          May prove a beauteous flower when next we meet.
          Good night, good night! As sweet repose and rest
130   Come to thy heart as that within my breast!
    ROM: O, wilt thou leave me so unsatisfied?
    JUL: What satisfaction canst thou have to-night?
    ROM: Th' exchange of thy love's faithful vow for mine.
    JUL: I gave thee mine before thou didst request it;
135   And yet I would it were to give again.
    ROM: Would'st thou withdraw it? For what purpose, love?

JUL: But[22] to be frank, and give it thee again.
     And yet I wish but for the thing I have.
     My bounty is as boundless as the sea,
140 My love as deep; the more I give to thee,
     The more I have, for both are infinite.
     I hear some noise within. Dear love, adieu!
Nurse calls within.
     Anon, good nurse! Sweet Montague, be true.
     Stay but a little, I will come again.   *Exit.*
145 ROM: O blessed, blessed night! I am afeard,
     Being in night, all this is but a dream,
     Too flattering-sweet to be substantial.

Enter Juliet above.

JUL: Three words, dear Romeo, and good night indeed.
     If that thy bent of love be honourable,
150 Thy purpose marriage, send me word to-morrow,
     By one that I'll procure to come to thee,
     Where and what time thou wilt perform the rite;
     And all my fortunes at thy foot I'll lay
     And follow thee my lord throughout the world.
155 NURSE: *Within.*   Madam!
JUL: I come, anon.—But if thou meanest not well,
     I do beseech thee—
NURSE: *Within.*   Madam!
JUL: By-and-by, I come.—
160 To cease thy suit and leave me to my grief.
     To-morrow will I send.
ROM: So thrive my soul—
JUL: A thousand times good night!   *Exit.*
ROM: A thousand times the worse, to want thy light!
165 Love goes toward love as schoolboys from their books;
     But love from love, towards school with heavy looks.

Enter Juliet again, above.

JUL: Hist![23] Romeo, hist! O for a falconer's voice
     To lure this tassel-gentle back again!
     Bondage is hoarse and may not speak aloud;

[22]*only*

[23]*[Juliet is trying to call Romeo back without making noise]*

170   Else would I tear the cave where Echo lies,
And make her airy tongue more hoarse than mine
With repetition of my Romeo's name.
Romeo!

ROM: It is my soul that calls upon my name.

175   How silver-sweet sound lovers' tongues by night,
Like softest music to attending ears!

JUL: Romeo!

ROM: My dear?

JUL: What o'clock to-morrow

180   Shall I send to thee?

ROM: By the hour of nine.

JUL: I will not fail. 'Tis twenty years till then.
I have forgot why I did call thee back.

ROM: Let me stand here till thou remember it.

185 JUL: I shall forget, to have thee still stand there,
Remembering how I love thy company.

ROM: And I'll still stay, to have thee still forget,
Forgetting any other home but this.

JUL: 'Tis almost morning. I would have thee gone—

190   And yet no farther than a wanton's[24] bird,
That lets it hop a little from her hand,
Like a poor prisoner in his twisted gyves,[25]
And with a silk thread plucks it back again,
So loving-jealous of his liberty.

195 ROM: I would I were thy bird.

JUL: Sweet, so would I.
Yet I should kill thee with much cherishing.
Good night, good night! Parting is such sweet sorrow,
That I shall say good night till it be morrow.   *Exit.*

200 ROM: Sleep dwell upon thine eyes, peace in thy breast!
Would I were sleep and peace, so sweet to rest!
Hence will I to my ghostly father's cell,
His help to crave and my dear hap to tell.   *Exit.*

[24]*prostitute's*

[25]*shackles*

SCENE III
Friar Laurence's cell.

Enter Friar Laurence alone, with a basket.

FRIAR: The grey-ey'd morn smiles on the frowning night,
    Check'ring the Eastern clouds with streaks of light;
    And flecked darkness like a drunkard reels
    From forth day's path and Titan's fiery wheels.[26]
5   Now, ere[27] the sun advance his burning eye
    The day to cheer and night's dank dew to dry,
    I must up-fill this osier cage[28] of ours
    With baleful[29] weeds and precious-juiced[30] flowers.
    The earth that's nature's mother is her tomb.
10   What is her burying grave, that is her womb;
    And from her womb children of divers kind
    We sucking on her natural bosom find;
    Many for many virtues excellent,
    None but for some, and yet all different.
15   O, mickle[31] is the powerful grace that lies
    In plants, herbs, stones, and their true qualities;
    For naught so vile that on the earth doth live
    But to the earth some special good doth give;
    Nor aught so good but, strain'd from that fair use,
20   Revolts from true birth, stumbling on abuse.
    Virtue itself turns vice, being misapplied,
    And vice sometime's by action dignified.
    Within the infant rind of this small flower
    Poison hath residence, and medicine power;
25   For this, being smelt, with that part cheers each part;
    Being tasted, slays all senses with the heart.
    Two such opposed kings encamp them still
    In man as well as herbs—grace and rude will;
    And where the worser is predominant,
30   Full soon the canker death eats up that plant.

Enter Romeo.

ROM: Good morrow, father.
FRIAR: Benedicite![32]

[26] the chariot of Apollo, god of the sun

[27] before

[28] willow basket

[29] poisonous

[30] medicinal

[31] great, much

[32] God's blessing (Latin)

What early tongue so sweet saluteth me?

Young son, it argues a distempered[33] head

35   So soon to bid good morrow to thy bed.

Care keeps his watch in every old man's eye,

And where care lodges sleep will never lie;

But where unbruised youth with unstuff'd brain

Doth couch his limbs, there golden sleep doth reign.

40   Therefore thy earliness doth me assure

Thou art uprous'd with some distemp'rature;

Or if not so, then here I hit it right—

Our Romeo hath not been in bed to-night.

ROM: That last is true—the sweeter rest was mine.

45 FRIAR: God pardon sin! Wast thou with Rosaline?

ROM: With Rosaline, my ghostly[34] father? No.

I have forgot that name, and that name's woe.

FRIAR: That's my good son! But where hast thou been then?

ROM: I'll tell thee ere thou ask it me again.

50   I have been feasting with mine enemy,

Where on a sudden one hath wounded me

That's by me wounded. Both our remedies

Within thy help and holy physic lies.

I bear no hatred, blessed man, for, lo,

55   My intercession likewise steads my foe.

FRIAR: Be plain, good son, and homely in thy drift

Riddling confession finds but riddling shrift.

ROM: Then plainly know my heart's dear love is set

On the fair daughter of rich Capulet;

60   As mine on hers, so hers is set on mine,

And all combin'd, save what thou must combine

By holy marriage. When, and where, and how

We met, we woo'd, and made exchange of vow,

I'll tell thee as we pass; but this I pray,

65   That thou consent to marry us to-day.

FRIAR: Holy Saint Francis! What a change is here!

Is Rosaline, that thou didst love so dear,

So soon forsaken? Young men's love then lies

Not truly in their hearts, but in their eyes.

70   Jesu Maria! What a deal of brine[35]

Hath wash'd thy sallow cheeks for Rosaline!

How much salt water thrown away in waste,

[33]*off-balance, sick*

[34]*holy, spiritual*

[35]*saltwater; tears*

To season love, that of it doth not taste!
The sun not yet thy sighs from heaven clears,
75　Thy old groans ring yet in mine ancient ears.
Lo, here upon thy cheek the stain doth sit
Of an old tear that is not wash'd off yet.
If e'er thou wast thyself, and these woes thine,
Thou and these woes were all for Rosaline.
80　And art thou chang'd? Pronounce this sentence then:
Women may fall when there's no strength in men.

ROM:　Thou chid'st me oft for loving Rosaline.

FRIAR:　For doting,[36] not for loving, pupil mine.

ROM:　And bad'st me bury love.

85　FRIAR:　Not in a grave
To lay one in, another out to have.

ROM:　I pray thee chide not. She whom I love now
Doth grace for grace and love for love allow.
The other did not so.

90　FRIAR:　O, she knew well
Thy love did read by rote, and could not spell.
But come, young waverer, come go with me.
In one respect I'll thy assistant be;
For this alliance may so happy prove
95　To turn your households' rancour[37] to pure love.

ROM:　O, let us hence! I stand on sudden haste.

FRIAR:　Wisely, and slow. They stumble that run fast.

Exeunt.

[36]*being infatuated with*

[37]*bitterness*

SCENE IV
A Street.

Enter Benvolio and Mercutio.

MER: Where the devil should this Romeo be?
　　Came he not home to-night?

BEN: Not to his father's. I spoke with his man.

MER: Why, that same pale hard-hearted wench,
5　　that Rosaline, torments him so that he will sure run mad.

BEN: Tybalt, the kinsman to old Capulet,
　　Hath sent a letter to his father's house.

MER: A challenge, on my life.

BEN: Romeo will answer it.

10 MER: Any man that can write may answer a letter.

BEN: Nay, he will answer the letter's master, how he dares,
　　being dared.

MER: Alas, poor Romeo, he is already dead! stabb'd with
　　a white wench's black eye; shot through the ear with a
15　　love song; the very pin of his heart cleft with the blind
　　bow-boy's butt-shaft;[38] and is he a man to encounter
　　Tybalt?

BEN: Why, what is Tybalt?

MER: More than Prince of Cats, I can tell you. O, he's the
20　　courageous captain of compliments.[39] He fights as you
　　sing pricksong, keeps time, distance, and proportion;
　　rests me his minim rest, one, two, and the third in your
　　bosom! the very butcher of a silk button, a duellist, a
　　duellist! a gentle man of the very first house, of the first
25　　and second cause. Ah, the immortal passado! the punto
　　reverso! the hai![40]

BEN: The what?

MER: The pox of such antic, lisping, affecting
　　fantasticoes[41]—these new tuners of accent! 'By Jesu, a
30　　very good blade! a very tall man! a very good whore!'
　　Why, is not this a lamentable thing, grandsir, that we
　　should be thus afflicted with these strange flies, these
　　fashion-mongers, these pardona-me's, who stand so
　　much on the new form that they cannot sit at ease on
35　　the old bench? O, their bones, their bones!

[38]*Cupid's arrow*

[39]*one who knows all the rituals of dueling*

[40]*[fencing terms]*

[41]*effeminate men*

Enter Romeo.

BEN: Here comes Romeo! here comes Romeo!
MER: Without his roe,[42] like a dried herring. O flesh, flesh,
       how art thou fishified! Now is he for the numbers that
       Petrarch flowed in. Laura,[43] to his lady, was but a kitchen
40   wench (marry, she had a better love to berhyme her),
       Dido a dowdy, Cleopatra a gypsy, Helen and Hero hild-
       ings and harlots, Thisbe a gray eye or so, but not to the
       purpose. Signior Romeo, bon jour! There's a French salu-
       tation to your French slop. You gave us the counterfeit
45   fairly last night.
ROM: Good morrow to you both. What counterfeit did I give
       you?
MER: The slip, sir, the slip. Can you not conceive?
ROM: Pardon, good Mercutio. My business was great, and
50   in such a case as mine a man may strain courtesy.
MER: That's as much as to say, such a case as yours con-
       strains a man to bow in the hams.
ROM: Meaning, to curtsy.
MER: Thou hast most kindly hit it.
55 ROM: A most courteous exposition.
MER: Nay, I am the very pink of courtesy.
ROM: Pink for flower.
MER: Right.
ROM: Why, then is my pump[44] well-flower'd.
60 MER: Well said! Follow me this jest now till thou hast worn
       out thy pump, that, when the single sole of it is worn,
       the jest may remain, after the wearing, solely singular.
ROM: O single-sold jest, solely singular for the singleness!
MER: Come between us, good Benvolio! My wits faint.
65 ROM: Switch and spurs, switch and spurs! or I'll cry a match.
MER: Nay, if our wits run the wild-goose chase, I am done;
       for thou hast more of the wild goose in one of thy wits
       than, I am sure, I have in my whole five. Was I with you
       there for the goose?
70 ROM: Thou wast never with me for anything when thou
       wast not there for the goose.
MER: I will bite thee by the ear for that jest.
ROM: Nay, good goose, bite not!

[42]*fish eggs; Mercutio is saying Romeo is wasting away with love*

[43]*"Laura" was the name given by the Italian poet Petrarch to his beloved; for the rest of the women listed here, see glossary*

[44]*[Romeo puns that his shoe (pump) is decorated with flowery designs; Mercutio continues the pun on shoes]*

[45]stretchable goatskin; an "ell" is a measurement of almost four feet

[46]fool

MER: Thy wit is a very bitter sweeting; it is a most sharp
75   sauce.

ROM: And is it not, then, well serv'd in to a sweet goose?

MER: O, here's a wit of cheverel,[45] that stretches from an
     inch narrow to an ell broad!

ROM: I stretch it out for that word 'broad,' which, added to
80   the goose, proves thee far and wide a broad goose.

MER: Why, is not this better now than groaning for love?
     Now art thou sociable, now art thou Romeo; now art
     thou what thou art, by art as well as by nature. For this
     drivelling love is like a great natural[46] that runs lolling
85   up and down to hide his bauble in a hole.

BEN: Stop there, stop there!

MER: Thou desirest me to stop in my tale against the hair.

BEN: Thou wouldst else have made thy tale large.

MER: O, thou art deceiv'd! I would have made it short; for I
90   was come to the whole depth of my tale, and meant
     indeed to occupy the argument no longer.

ROM: Here's goodly gear!

Enter Nurse and her Man, Peter.

MER: A sail, a sail!

BEN: Two, two! a shirt and a smock.

95 NURSE: Peter!

PETER: Anon.

NURSE: My fan, Peter.

MER: Good Peter, to hide her face; for her fan's the fairer
     face of the two.

100 NURSE: God ye good morrow, gentlemen.

MER: God ye good-den, fair gentlewoman.

NURSE: Is it good-den?

MER: 'Tis no less, I tell ye; for the bawdy hand of the dial is
     now upon the prick of noon.

105 NURSE: Out upon you! What a man are you!

ROM: One, gentlewoman, that God hath made for himself
     to mar.

NURSE: By my troth, it is well said. 'For himself to mar,'
     quoth a? Gentlemen, can any of you tell me where I
110   may find the young Romeo?

ROM: I can tell you; but young Romeo will be older when
  you have found him than he was when you sought him. I
  am the youngest of that name, for fault of a worse.

NURSE: You say well.

115 MER: Yea, is the worst well? Very well took, i' faith! wisely,
  wisely.

NURSE: If you be he, sir, I desire some confidence[47] with you.

BEN: She will indite[47] him to some supper.

MER: A bawd, a bawd, a bawd! So ho!

120 ROM: What hast thou found?

MER: No hare, sir; unless a hare, sir, in a lenten pie, that is
  something stale and hoar ere it be spent.

He walks by them and sings.

      An old hare hoar,
      And an old hare hoar,
125   Is very good meat in Lent;
      But a hare that is hoar
      Is too much for a score
      When it hoars ere it be spent.

  Romeo, will you come to your father's? We'll to dinner
130   thither.

ROM: I will follow you.

MER: Farewell, ancient Lady. Farewell,   *Sings*
  lady, lady, lady.   *Exeunt Mercutio, Benvolio.*

NURSE: Marry, farewell! I pray you, sir, what saucy merchant
  was this that was so full of his ropery?[48]

135 ROM: A gentleman, nurse, that loves to hear himself talk and
  will speak more in a minute than he will stand to in a
  month.

NURSE: An' a speak anything against me, I'll take him down,
  an' a were lustier than he is, and twenty such jacks; and
140   if I cannot, I'll find those that shall. Scurvy knave! I am
  none of his flirt-gills; I am none of his skains-mates. And
  thou must stand by too, and suffer every knave to use me
  at his pleasure!

PETER: I saw no man use you at his pleasure. If I had, my
145   weapon should quickly have been out, I warrant you. I
  dare draw as soon as another man, if I see occasion in a
  good quarrel, and the law on my side.

NURSE: Now, afore God, I am so vexed that every part about

[47]*the nurse's mistake for "conference"; Benvolio mocks her by using "indite" for "invite."*

[48]*ribaldry*

me quivers. Scurvy knave! Pray you, sir, a word; and, as
150   I told you, my young lady bid me enquire you out.
What she bid me say, I will keep to myself; but first let
me tell ye, if ye should lead her into a fool's paradise, as
they say, it were a very gross kind of behaviour, as they
say; for the gentle woman is young; and there-fore, if
155   you should deal double with her, truly it were an ill
thing to be off'red to any gentlewoman, and very weak
dealing.

ROM: Nurse, commend me to thy lady and mistress. I protest unto thee—

160 NURSE: Good heart, and i' faith I will tell her as much.
Lord, Lord! she will be a joyful woman.

ROM: What wilt thou tell her, nurse? Thou dost not mark
me.

NURSE: I will tell her, sir, that you do protest, which, as I
165   take it, is a gentlemanlike offer.

ROM: Bid her devise some means to come to shrift
This afternoon;
And there she shall at Friar Laurence' cell
Be shriv'd and married. Here is for thy pains.

170 NURSE: No, truly, sir; not a penny.

ROM: Go to! I say you shall.

NURSE: This afternoon, sir? Well, she shall be there.

ROM: And stay, good nurse, behind the abbey wall.
Within this hour my man shall be with thee
175   And bring thee cords made like a tackled stair,
Which to the high topgallant of my joy
Must be my convoy in the secret night.
Farewell. Be trusty, and I'll quit thy pains.
Farewell. Commend me to thy mistress.

180 NURSE: Now God in heaven bless thee! Hark you, sir.

ROM: What say'st thou, my dear nurse?

NURSE: Is your man secret? Did you ne'er hear say,
Two may keep counsel, putting one away?

ROM: I warrant thee my man's as true as steel.

185 NURSE: Well, sir, my mistress is the sweetest lady. Lord,
Lord! when 'twas a little prating thing—O, there is a
nobleman in town, one Paris, that would fain lay knife
aboard; but she, good soul, had as lieve see a toad, a

190 very toad, as see him. I anger her sometimes, and tell her
that Paris is the properer man; but I'll warrant you, when
I say so, she looks as pale as any clout in the   versal
world. Doth not rosemary and Romeo begin both with a
letter?

ROM: Ay, nurse; what of that? Both with an R.

195 NURSE: Ah, mocker! that's the dog's name. R is for the—No; I
know it begins with some other letter; and she hath the
prettiest sententious of it, of you and rosemary, that it
would do you good to hear it.

ROM: Commend me to thy lady.

200 NURSE: Ay, a thousand times.   *Exit Romeo.*   Peter!

PETER: Anon.

NURSE: Peter, take my fan, and go before, and apace.

Exeunt.

SCENE V
Capulet's orchard.

Enter Juliet.

JUL: The clock struck nine when I did send the nurse;
In half an hour she promis'd to return.
Perchance she cannot meet him. That's not so.
O, she is lame! Love's heralds should be thoughts,
5   Which ten times faster glide than the sun's beams
Driving back shadows over low'ring hills.
Therefore do nimble-pinion'd doves draw Love,
And therefore hath the wind-swift Cupid wings.
Now is the sun upon the highmost hill
10   Of this day's journey, and from nine till twelve
Is three long hours; yet she is not come.
Had she affections and warm youthful blood,
She would be as swift in motion as a ball;
My words would bandy her to my sweet love,
15   And his to me,
But old folks, many feign[49] as they were dead—
Unwieldy, slow, heavy and pale as lead.

[49]*pretend*

Enter Nurse and Peter.

          O God, she comes! O honey nurse, what news?

          Hast thou met with him? Send thy man away.

20 NURSE: Peter, stay at the gate.   *Exit Peter.*

      JUL: Now, good sweet nurse—O Lord, why look'st thou

          sad?

          Though news be sad, yet tell them merrily;

          If good, thou shamest the music of sweet news

25   By playing it to me with so sour a face.

      NURSE: I am aweary, give me leave awhile.

          Fie, how my bones ache! What a jaunt have I had!

      JUL: I would thou hadst my bones, and I thy news.

          Nay, come, I pray thee speak. Good, good nurse, speak.

30 NURSE: Jesu, what haste! Can you not stay awhile?

          Do you not see that I am out of breath?

      JUL: How art thou out of breath when thou hast breath

          To say to me that thou art out of breath?

          The excuse that thou dost make in this delay

35   Is longer than the tale thou dost excuse.

          Is thy news good or bad? Answer to that.

          Say either, and I'll stay the circumstance.[50]

          Let me be satisfied, is't good or bad?

      NURSE: Well, you have made a simple choice; you know

40   not how to choose a man. Romeo? No, not he. Though

          his face be better than any man's, yet his leg excels all

          men's; and for a hand and a foot, and a body, though

          they be not to be talk'd on, yet they are past compare.

          He is not the flower of courtesy, but, I'll warrant him,

45   as gentle as a lamb. Go thy ways, wench; serve God.

          What, have you din'd at home?

      JUL: No, no. But all this did I know before.

          What says he of our marriage? What of that?

      NURSE: Lord, how my head aches! What a head have I!

50   It beats as it would fall in twenty pieces.

          My back o' t' other side,—ah, my back, my back!

          Beshrew your heart for sending me about

          To catch my death with jaunting up and down!

      JUL: I' faith, I am sorry that thou art not well.

55   Sweet, sweet, sweet nurse, tell me, what says my love?

      NURSE: Your love says, like an honest gentleman, and a

[50]handle the situation

courteous, and a kind, and a handsome; and, I warrant,
a virtuous—Where is your mother?

JUL: Where is my mother? Why, she is within.

60   Where should she be? How oddly thou reply'st!
'Your love says, like an honest gentleman,
"Where is your mother?"'

NURSE: O God's Lady dear!
Are you so hot? Marry come up, I trow.

65   Is this the poultice for my aching bones?
Henceforward do your messages yourself.

JUL: Here's such a coil! Come, what says Romeo?

NURSE: Have you got leave to go to shrift to-day?

JUL: I have.

70 NURSE: Then hie you hence to Friar Laurence' cell;
There stays a husband to make you a wife.
Now comes the wanton blood[51] up in your cheeks:
They'll be in scarlet straight at any news.
Hie you to church; I must another way,

75   To fetch a ladder, by the which your love
Must climb a bird's nest soon when it is dark.
I am the drudge, and toil in your delight;
But you shall bear the burden soon at night.
Go; I'll to dinner; hie you to the cell.[52]

80 JUL: Hie to high fortune! Honest nurse, farewell.

                              Exeunt.

[51] *unmaidenly blush*

[52] *Friar Laurence's residence*

SCENE VI
Friar Laurence's cell.

Enter Friar Laurence and Romeo.

FRIAR: So smile the heavens upon this holy act
That after-hours with sorrow chide us not!

ROM: Amen, amen! But come what sorrow can,
It cannot countervail the exchange of joy

5   That one short minute gives me in her sight.
Do thou but close our hands with holy words,
Then love-devouring death do what he dare—
It is enough I may but call her mine.

FRIAR: These violent delights have violent ends
10   And in their triumph die, like fire and powder,
          Which, as they kiss, consume. The sweetest honey
          Is loathsome in his own deliciousness
          And in the taste confounds the appetite.
          Therefore love moderately: long love doth so;
15   Too swift arrives as tardy as too slow.
     Enter Juliet.
          Here comes the Lady. O, so light a foot
          Will ne'er wear out the everlasting flint.
          A lover may bestride the gossamer[53]
          That idles in the wanton[54] summer air,
20   And yet not fall; so light is vanity.[55]
     JUL: Good even to my ghostly confessor.
     FRIAR: Romeo shall thank thee, daughter, for us both.
     JUL: As much to him, else is his thanks too much.
     ROM: Ah, Juliet, if the measure of thy joy
25   Be heap'd like mine, and that thy skill be more
          To blazon[56] it, then sweeten with thy breath
          This neighbour air, and let rich music's tongue
          Unfold the imagin'd happiness that both
          Receive in either by this dear encounter.
30   JUL: Conceit,[57] more rich in matter than in words,
          Brags of his substance, not of ornament.
          They are but beggars that can count their worth;
          But my true love is grown to such excess,
          I cannot sum up sum of half my wealth.
35   FRIAR: Come, come with me, and we will make short work;
          For, by your leaves, you shall not stay alone
          Till Holy Church incorporate two in one.
                                        Exeunt.

[53]*fine thread, spiderweb*

[54]*playful, uninhibited*

[55]*useless pursuit of earthly pleasures*

[56]*trumpet*

[57]*understanding*

ACT III

SCENE I
A public place.

Enter Mercutio, Benvolio, and Men.

BEN: I pray thee, good Mercutio, let's retire.
    The day is hot, the Capulets abroad.
    And if we meet, we shall not scape a brawl,
    For now, these hot days, is the mad blood stirring.
5 MER: Thou art like one of these fellows that, when he enters
    the confines of a tavern, claps me his sword upon the
    table and says 'God send me no need of thee!' and by the
    operation of the second cup draws him on the drawer,
10   when indeed there is no need.
BEN: Am I like such a fellow?
MER: Come, come, thou art as hot a jack in thy mood as any
    in Italy; and as soon moved to be moody, and as soon
    moody to be moved.
15 BEN: And what to?
MER: Nay, an[1] there were two such, we should have none   [1]*If*
    shortly, for one would kill the other. Thou! why, thou
    wilt quarrel with a man that hath a hair more or a hair
    less in his beard than thou hast. Thou wilt quarrel with a
20   man for cracking nuts, having no other reason but be-
    cause thou hast hazel eyes. What eye but such an eye
    would spy out such a quarrel? Thy head is as full of quar
    rels as an egg is full of meat; and yet thy head hath been
    beaten as addle as an egg for quarrelling. Thou hast quar-
25   rell'd with a man for coughing in the street, because he
    hath wakened thy dog that hath lain asleep in the sun.
    Didst thou not fall out with a tailor for wearing his new
    doublet before Easter, with another for tying his new

shoes with an old riband? And yet thou wilt tutor me
30   from quarrelling!

BEN: An I were so apt to quarrel as thou art, any man
     should buy the fee simple[2] of my life for an hour and a
     quarter.

MER: The fee simple? O simple!

Enter Tybalt and others.

35 **BEN:** By my head, here come the Capulets.

MER: By my heel, I care not.

TYB: Follow me close, for I will speak to them.
     Gentlemen, good den. A word with one of you.

MER: And but one word with one of us?
40   Couple it with something; make it a word and a blow.

TYB: You shall find me apt enough to that, sir, an you will
     give me occasion.

MER: Could you not take some occasion without giving?

TYB: Mercutio, thou consortest with Romeo.
45 **MER:** Consort? What, dost thou make us minstrels? An
     thou make minstrels of us, look to hear nothing but
     discords. Here's my fiddlestick; here's that shall make
     you dance. Zounds,[3] consort!

BEN: We talk here in the public haunt of men.
50   Either withdraw unto some private place
     And reason coldly of your grievances,
     Or else depart. Here all eyes gaze on us.

MER: Men's eyes were made to look, and let them gaze.
     I will not budge for no man's pleasure, I.

Enter Romeo.

55 **TYB:** Well, peace be with you, sir. Here comes my man.

MER: But I'll be hang'd, sir, if he wear your livery.
     Marry, go before to field, he'll be your follower!
     Your worship in that sense may call him man.

TYB: Romeo, the love I bear thee can afford
60   No better term than this: thou art a villain.

ROM: Tybalt, the reason that I have to love thee
     Doth much excuse the appertaining[4] rage

---

[2]*unconditional ownership*

[3]*by Jesus' wounds [an oath]*

[4]*appropriate*

To such a greeting. Villain am I none.
Therefore farewell. I see thou knowest me not.

65　TYB: Boy, this shall not excuse the injuries
　　　　That thou hast done me; therefore turn and draw.

　　ROM: I do protest I never injur'd thee,
　　　　But love thee better than thou canst devise
　　　　Till thou shalt know the reason of my love;

70　　　　And so good Capulet, which name I tender
　　　　As dearly as mine own, be satisfied.

　　MER: O calm, dishonourable, vile submission!
　　　　Alla stoccata[5] carries it away.　　　　*Draws.*
　　　　Tybalt, you ratcatcher, will you walk?

75　TYB: What would'st thou have with me?

　　MER: Good King of Cats, nothing but one of your nine lives.
　　　　That I mean to make bold withal, and, as you shall use
　　　　me hereafter, dry-beat the rest of the eight. Will you
　　　　pluck your sword out of his pitcher by the ears? Make

80　　　　haste, lest mine be about your ears ere it be out.

　　TYB: I am for you.　　　　　　　　　*Draws.*

　　ROM: Gentle Mercutio, put thy rapier up.

　　MER: Come, sir, your passado!　　　*They fight.*

　　ROM: Draw, Benvolio; beat down their weapons.

85　　　　Gentlemen, for shame! forbear this outrage!
　　　　Tybalt, Mercutio, the Prince expressly hath
　　　　Forbid this bandying in Verona streets.
　　　　Hold, Tybalt! Good Mercutio!

Tybalt under Romeo's arm thrusts Mercutio in, and flies with his Followers.

　　MER: I am hurt.

90　　　　A plague o' both your houses! I am sped.
　　　　Is he gone and hath nothing?

　　BEN: What, art thou hurt?

　　MER: Ay, ay, a scratch, a scratch. Marry, 'tis enough.
　　　　Where is my page? Go, villain, fetch a surgeon.
　　　　　　　　　　　　　　　　　　Exit Page.

95　ROM: Courage, man. The hurt cannot be much.

　　MER: No, 'tis not so deep as a well, nor so wide as a church
　　　　door; but 'tis enough, 'twill serve. Ask for me to-morrow,

[5] *a thrust of the sword*

and you shall find me a grave man. I am peppered, I
warrant, for this world. A plague o' both your houses!
100   Zounds, a dog, a rat, a mouse, a cat, to scratch a man to
death! a braggart, a rogue, a villain, that fights by the
book of arithmetic! Why the devil came you between
us? I was hurt under your arm.

ROM: I thought all for the best.

105 MER: Help me into some house, Benvolio,
Or I shall faint. A plague o' both your houses!
They have made worms' meat of me. I have it,
And soundly too. Your houses!

Exit, supported by Benvolio.

ROM: This gentleman, the Prince's near ally,
110   My very friend, hath got this mortal hurt
In my behalf—my reputation stain'd
With Tybalt's slander—Tybalt, that an hour
Hath been my kinsman. O sweet Juliet,
Thy beauty hath made me effeminate
115   And in my temper soft'ned valour's steel

Enter Benvolio.

BEN: O Romeo, Romeo, brave Mercutio's dead!

6climped up to

That gallant spirit hath aspir'd[6] the clouds,
Which too untimely here did scorn the earth.
120 ROM: This day's black fate on more days doth depend;
This but begins the woe others must end.

Enter Tybalt.

BEN: Here comes the furious Tybalt back again.
ROM: Alive in triumph, and Mercutio slain?
Away to heaven respective lenity,
125   And fire-ey'd fury be my conduct now!
Now, Tybalt, take the 'villain' back again
That late thou gavest me; for Mercutio's soul
Is but a little way above our heads,
Staying for thine to keep him company.
130   Either thou or I, or both, must go with him.

TYB:　Thou, wretched boy, that didst consort him here,
　　　Shalt with him hence.
ROM:　This shall determine that.　　*They fight. Tybalt falls.*
BEN:　Romeo, away, be gone!
135　　The citizens are up, and Tybalt slain.
　　　Stand not amaz'd. The Prince will doom thee death
　　　If thou art taken. Hence, be gone, away!
ROM:　O, I am fortune's fool!
BEN:　Why dost thou stay?　　　　　*Exit Romeo.*

Enter Citizens.

140　CITIZEN:　Which way ran he that kill'd Mercutio?
　　　Tybalt, that murderer, which way ran he?
BEN:　There lies that Tybalt.
CITIZEN:　Up, sir, go with me.
　　　I charge thee in the Prince's name obey.

Enter Prince (attended), Old Montague, Capulet, their Wives,
and others.

145　PRINCE:　Where are the vile beginners of this fray?
BEN:　O noble Prince, I can discover all
　　　The unlucky manage of this fatal brawl.
　　　There lies the man, slain by young Romeo,
　　　That slew thy kinsman, brave Mercutio.
150　LADY CAP:　Tybalt, my cousin! O my brother's child!
　　　O Prince! O husband! O, the blood is spill'd
　　　Of my dear kinsman! Prince, as thou art true,
　　　For blood of ours, shed blood of Montague.
　　　O cousin, cousin!
155　PRINCE:　Benvolio, who began this bloody fray?
BEN:　Tybalt, here slain, whom Romeo's hand did slay.
　　　Romeo, that spoke him fair, bid him bethink
　　　How nice the quarrel was, and urg'd withal
　　　Your high displeasure. All this, uttered
160　　With gentle breath, calm look, knees humbly bow'd,
　　　Could not take truce with the unruly spleen
　　　Of Tybalt deaf to peace, but that he tilts
　　　With piercing steel at bold Mercutio's breast;

Who, all as hot, turns deadly point to point,
165 And, with a martial scorn, with one hand beats
Cold death aside and with the other sends
It back to Tybalt, whose dexterity
Retorts it. Romeo he cries aloud,
'Hold, friends! friends, part!' and swifter than his
170   tongue,
His agile arm beats down their fatal points,
And 'twixt them rushes; underneath whose arm
An envious thrust from Tybalt hit the life
Of stout Mercutio, and then Tybalt fled;
175 But by-and-by comes back to Romeo,
Who had but newly entertain'd revenge,
And to't they go like lightning; for, ere I
Could draw to part them, was stout Tybalt slain;
And, as he fell, did Romeo turn and fly.
180 This is the truth, or let Benvolio die.

LADY CAP: He is a kinsman to the Montague;
Affection makes him false, he speaks not true.
Some twenty of them fought in this black strife,
And all those twenty could but kill one life.
185 I beg for justice, which thou, Prince, must give.
Romeo slew Tybalt; Romeo must not live.

PRINCE: Romeo slew him; he slew Mercutio.
Who now the price of his dear blood doth owe?

MON: Not Romeo, Prince; he was Mercutio's friend;
190 His fault concludes but what the law should end,
The life of Tybalt.

PRINCE: And for that offence
Immediately we do exile him hence.
I have an interest in your hate's proceeding,
195 My blood for your rude brawls doth lie ableeding;
But I'll amerce[7] you with so strong a fine
That you shall all repent the loss of mine.
I will be deaf to pleading and excuses;
Nor tears nor prayers shall purchase out abuses.
200 Therefore use none. Let Romeo hence in haste,
Else, when he is found, that hour is his last.
Bear hence this body, and attend our will.
Mercy but murders, pardoning those that kill.[8]   *Exeunt.*

[7]*punish*

[8]*i.e., Pardoning those who kill causes more murders.*

SCENE II
Capulet's orchard.

Enter Juliet alone.

JUL: Gallop apace, you fiery-footed steeds,
      Towards Phoebus'[9] lodging! Such a wagoner
      As Phaeton would whip you to the west
      And bring in cloudy night immediately.
5   Spread thy close curtain, love-performing night,
      That runaway eyes may wink, and Romeo
      Leap to these arms untalk'd of and unseen.
      Lovers can see to do their amorous rites
10   By their own beauties; or, if love be blind,
      It best agrees with night. Come, civil night,
      Thou sober-suited matron, all in black,
      And learn me how to lose a winning match,
      Play'd for a pair of stainless maidenhoods.
15   Hood my unmann'd blood, bating in my cheeks,
      With thy black mantle till strange love, grown bold,
      Think true love acted simple modesty.
      Come, night; come, Romeo, come, thou day in night;
      For thou wilt lie upon the wings of night
20   Whiter than new snow upon a raven's back.
      Come, gentle night; come, loving, black-brow'd night;
      Give me my Romeo; and, when he shall die,
      Take him and cut him out in little stars,
      And he will make the face of heaven so fine
25   That all the world will be in love with night
      And pay no worship to the garish sun.
      O, I have bought the mansion of a love,
      But not possess'd it; and though I am sold,
      Not yet enjoy'd. So tedious is this day
30   As is the night before some festival
      To an impatient child that hath new robes
      And may not wear them. O, here comes my nurse,
      And she brings news; and every tongue that speaks
      But Romeo's name speaks heavenly eloquence.
      Enter Nurse, with cords.
35   Now, nurse, what news? What hast thou there? the cords[10]
      That Romeo bid thee fetch?

[9]another name for Apollo, god of the sun; Phaeton, Apollo's son, once drove the sun across the sky

[10]rope ladder

NURSE: Ay, ay, the cords.   *Throws them down.*

JUL: Ay me! what news? Why dost thou wring thy hands?

NURSE: Ah, well-a-day! he's dead, he's dead, he's dead!

40   We are undone, lady, we are undone!

Alack the day! he's gone, he's kill'd, he's dead!

JUL: Can heaven be so envious?

NURSE: Romeo can,

Though heaven cannot. O Romeo, Romeo!

45   Who ever would have thought it? Romeo!

JUL: What devil art thou that dost torment me thus?

This torture should be roar'd in dismal hell.

Hath Romeo slain himself? Say thou but 'I,'

And that bare vowel 'I' shall poison more

11 fabled serpent that killed with its eyes

50   Than the death-darting eye of cockatrice.[11]

I am not I, if there be such an 'I';

Or those eyes shut that make thee answer 'I.'

If he be slain, say 'I'; or if not, 'no.'

Brief sounds determine of my weal or woe.

55 NURSE: I saw the wound, I saw it with mine eyes,

(God save the mark!) here on his manly breast.

A piteous corse, a bloody piteous corse;

Pale, pale as ashes, all bedaub'd in blood,

All in gore-blood. I swounded at the sight.

60 JUL: O, break, my heart! poor bankrout, break at once!

To prison, eyes; ne'er look on liberty!

Vile earth, to earth resign; end motion here,

And thou and Romeo press one heavy bier!

NURSE: O Tybalt, Tybalt, the best friend I had!

65   O courteous Tybalt! honest gentleman

That ever I should live to see thee dead!

JUL: What storm is this that blows so contrary?

Is Romeo slaught'red, and is Tybalt dead?

My dear-lov'd cousin, and my dearer lord?

70   Then, dreadful trumpet, sound the general doom!

For who is living, if those two are gone?

NURSE: Tybalt is gone, and Romeo banished;

Romeo that kill'd him, he is banished.

JUL: O God! Did Romeo's hand shed Tybalt's blood?

75 NURSE: It did, it did! alas the day, it did!

JUL: O serpent heart, hid with a flow'ring face!

Did ever dragon keep so fair a cave?
Beautiful tyrant! fiend angelical!
Dove-feather'd raven! wolvish-ravening lamb!
80   Despised substance of divinest show!
Just opposite to what thou justly seem'st—
A damned saint, an honourable villain!
O nature, what hadst thou to do in hell
When thou didst bower[12] the spirit of a fiend

85   In mortal paradise of such sweet flesh?
Was ever book containing such vile matter
So fairly bound? O, that deceit should dwell
In such a gorgeous palace!
NURSE: There's no trust,
90   No faith, no honesty in men; all perjur'd,
All forsworn, all naught, all dissemblers.
Ah, where's my man? Give me some aqua vitae.[13]
These griefs, these woes, these sorrows make me old.
Shame come to Romeo!

95 JUL: Blister'd be thy tongue
For such a wish! He was not born to shame.
Upon his brow shame is asham'd to sit;
For 'tis a throne where honour may be crown'd
Sole monarch of the universal earth.
100   O, what a beast was I to chide at him!
NURSE: Will you speak well of him that kill'd your cousin?
JUL: Shall I speak ill of him that is my husband?
Ah, poor my lord, what tongue shall smooth thy name
When I, thy three-hours' wife, have mangled it?
105   But wherefore, villain, didst thou kill my cousin?
That villain cousin would have kill'd my husband.
Back, foolish tears, back to your native spring!
Your tributary drops belong to woe,
Which you, mistaking, offer up to joy.
110   My husband lives, that Tybalt would have slain;
And Tybalt's dead, that would have slain my husband.
All this is comfort; wherefore weep I then?
Some word there was, worser than Tybalt's death,
That murdered me. I would forget it fain;
115   But O, it presses to my memory
Like damned guilty deeds to sinners' minds!

'Tybalt is dead, and Romeo banished.'
That 'banished,' that one word 'banished,'
Hath slain ten thousand Tybalts. Tybalt's death
120   Was woe enough, if it had ended there;
Or, if sour woe delights in fellowship
And needly will be[14] rank'd with other griefs,
Why followed not, when she said 'Tybalt's dead,'
Thy father, or thy mother, nay, or both,
125   Which modern lamentation might have mov'd?
But with a rearward following Tybalt's death,
'Romeo is banished'—to speak that word
Is father, mother, Tybalt, Romeo, Juliet,
All slain, all dead. 'Romeo is banished'—
130   There is no end, no limit, measure, bound,
In that word's death; no words can that woe sound.
Where is my father and my mother, nurse?
NURSE: Weeping and wailing over Tybalt's corse.
Will you go to them? I will bring you thither.
135 JUL: Wash they his wounds with tears? Mine shall be spent,
When theirs are dry, for Romeo's banishment.
Take up those cords. Poor ropes, you are beguil'd,
Both you and I, for Romeo is exil'd.
He made you for a highway to my bed;
140   But I, a maid, die maiden-widowed.
Come, cords; come, Nurse. I'll to my wedding bed;
And death, not Romeo, take my maidenhead!
NURSE: Hie to your chamber. I'll find Romeo
To comfort you. I wot[15] well where he is.
145   Hark ye, your Romeo will be here at night.
I'll to him; he is hid at Laurence' cell.
JUL: O, find him! give this ring to my true knight
And bid him come to take his last farewell.
                                             Exeunt.

[14]*needs to be*

[15]*know*

SCENE III
Friar Laurence's Cell.

Enter Friar Laurence.

FRIAR: Romeo, come forth; come forth, thou fearful man.
    Affliction is enamour'd[16] of thy parts,
    And thou art wedded to calamity.

Enter Romeo.

ROM: Father, what news? What is the Prince's doom?
5   What sorrow craves acquaintance at my hand
    That I yet know not?
FRIAR: Too familiar
    Is my dear son with such sour company.
    I bring thee tidings of the Prince's doom.
10 ROM: What less than doomsday is the Prince's doom?
FRIAR: A gentler judgment vanish'd[17] from his lips—
    Not body's death, but body's banishment.
ROM: Ha, banishment? Be merciful, say 'death';
    For exile hath more terror in his look,
15   Much more than death. Do not say 'banishment.'
FRIAR: Hence from Verona art thou banished.
    Be patient, for the world is broad and wide.
ROM: There is no world without Verona walls,
    But purgatory, torture, hell itself.
20   Hence banished is banish'd from the world,
    And world's exile is death. Then 'banishment'
    Is death misterm'd. Calling death 'banishment,'
    Thou cut'st my head off with a golden axe
    And smilest upon the stroke that murders me.
25 FRIAR: O deadly sin! O rude unthankfulness!
    Thy fault our law calls death; but the kind Prince,
    Taking thy part, hath rush'd[18] aside the law,
    And turn'd that black word death to banishment.
    This is dear mercy, and thou seest it not.
30 ROM: 'Tis torture, and not mercy. Heaven is here,
    Where Juliet lives; and every cat and dog
    And little mouse, every unworthy thing,

[16]*loving*

[17]*escaped into the air*

[18]*brushed*

Live here in heaven and may look on her;
But Romeo may not. More validity,
35   More honourable state, more courtship lives
In carrion flies than Romeo. They may seize
On the white wonder of dear Juliet's hand
And steal immortal blessing from her lips,
Who, even in pure and vestal modesty,
40   Still blush, as thinking their own kisses sin;
But Romeo may not—he is banished.
This may flies do, when I from this must fly;
They are free men, but I am banished.
And sayest thou yet that exile is not death?
45   Hadst thou no poison mix'd, no sharp-ground knife,
No sudden mean of death, though ne'er so mean,
But 'banished' to kill me—'banished'?
O friar, the damned use that word in hell;
Howling attends it! How hast thou the heart,
50   Being a divine, a ghostly confessor,
A sin-absolver, and my friend profess'd,
To mangle me with that word 'banished'?
FRIAR: Thou fond mad man, hear me a little speak.
ROM: O, thou wilt speak again of banishment.
55   FRIAR: I'll give thee armour to keep off that word;
Adversity's sweet milk, philosophy,
To comfort thee, though thou art banished.
ROM: Yet 'banished'? Hang up philosophy!
Unless philosophy can make a Juliet,
60   Displant a town, reverse a prince's doom,
It helps not, it prevails not. Talk no more.
FRIAR: O, then I see that madmen have no ears.
ROM: How should they, when that wise men have no eyes?
FRIAR: Let me dispute with thee of thy estate.[19]
65   ROM: Thou canst not speak of that thou dost not feel.
Wert thou as young as I, Juliet thy love,
An hour but married, Tybalt murdered,
Doting like me, and like me banished,
Then mightst thou speak, then mightst thou tear thy hair,
70   And fall upon the ground, as I do now,
Taking the measure of an unmade grave.

Knock within.

[19]*Let me convince you of your condition.*

FRIAR: Arise; one knocks. Good Romeo, hide thyself.

ROM: Not I; unless the breath of heartsick groans,

　　Mist-like infold me from the search of eyes.　　*Knock.*

75　FRIAR: Hark, how they knock! Who's there? Romeo, arise;

　　Thou wilt be taken.—Stay awhile!—Stand up;　　*Knock.*

　　Run to my study.—By-and-by!—God's will,

　　What simpleness is this.—I come, I come!　　*Knock.*

　　Who knocks so hard? Whence come you? What's your will?

80　NURSE: *Within.*　　Let me come in, and you shall know my

　　errand. I come from Lady Juliet.

FRIAR: Welcome, then.

Enter Nurse.

NURSE: O holy friar, O, tell me, holy friar,

　　Where is my lady's lord, where's Romeo?

85　FRIAR: There on the ground, with his own tears made drunk.

NURSE: O, he is even in my mistress' case,

　　Just in her case!

FRIAR: O woeful sympathy!

　　Piteous predicament!

90　NURSE: Even so lies she,

　　Blubbering and weeping, weeping and blubbering.

　　Stand up, stand up! Stand, an you be a man.

　　For Juliet's sake, for her sake, rise and stand!

　　Why should you fall into so deep an O?[20]

95　ROM: *Rises.*　　Nurse—

NURSE: Ah sir! ah sir! Well, death's the end of all.

ROM: Spakest thou of Juliet? How is it with her?

　　Doth not she think me an old murderer,

　　Now I have stain'd the childhood of our joy

100　With blood remov'd but little from her own?

　　Where is she? and how doth she? and what says

　　My conceal'd lady to our cancell'd love?

NURSE: O, she says nothing, sir, but weeps and weeps;

　　And now falls on her bed, and then starts up,

105　And Tybalt calls; and then on Romeo cries,

　　And then down falls again.

ROM: As if that name,

　　Shot from the deadly level of a gun,

[20]*heavy sigh, groan*

Did murder her; as that name's cursed hand
110   Murdered her kinsman. O, tell me, friar, tell me,
In what vile part of this anatomy
Doth my name lodge? Tell me, that I may sack
The hateful mansion.   *Draws his dagger.*
        FRIAR: Hold thy desperate hand.
115   Art thou a man? Thy form cries out thou art;
Thy tears are womanish, thy wild acts denote
The unreasonable fury of a beast.
Unseemly woman in a seeming man!
Or ill-beseeming beast in seeming both!
120   Thou hast amaz'd me. By my holy order,
I thought thy disposition better temper'd.
Hast thou slain Tybalt? Wilt thou slay thyself?
And slay thy lady that in thy life lives,
By doing damned hate upon thyself?
125   Why railest thou on thy birth, the heaven, and earth?
Since birth and heaven and earth, all three do meet
In thee at once; which thou at once wouldst lose.
Fie, fie, thou shamest thy shape, thy love, thy wit,
Which, like a usurer, abound'st in all,
130   And usest none in that true use indeed
Which should bedeck thy shape, thy love, thy wit.
Thy noble shape is but a form of wax
Digressing from the valour of a man;
Thy dear love sworn but hollow perjury,
135   Killing that love which thou hast vow'd to cherish;
Thy wit, that ornament to shape and love,
Misshapen in the conduct of them both,
Like powder in a skilless soldier's flask,
Is set afire by thine own ignorance,
140   And thou dismemb'red with thine own defence.
What, rouse thee, man! Thy Juliet is alive,
For whose dear sake thou wast but lately dead.
There art thou happy. Tybalt would kill thee,
But thou slewest Tybalt. There art thou happy too.
145   The law, that threat'ned death, becomes thy friend
And turns it to exile. There art thou happy.
A pack of blessings light upon thy back;
Happiness courts thee in her best array;

But, like a misbhav'd and sullen wench,
150 Thou pout'st upon thy fortune and thy love.
Take heed, take heed, for such die miserable.
Go get thee to thy love, as was decreed,
Ascend her chamber, hence and comfort her.
But look thou stay not till the watch be set,
155 For then thou canst not pass to Mantua,
Where thou shalt live till we can find a time
To blaze[21] your marriage, reconcile your friends,   [21]*make known*
Beg pardon of the Prince, and call thee back
With twenty hundred thousand times more joy
160 Than thou went'st forth in lamentation.
Go before, Nurse. Commend me to thy lady,
And bid her hasten all the house to bed,
Which heavy sorrow makes them apt unto.
Romeo is coming.
165 NURSE: O Lord, I could have stay'd here all the night
To hear good counsel. O, what learning is!
My lord, I'll tell my lady you will come.
ROM: Do so, and bid my sweet prepare to chide.
NURSE: Here is a ring she bid me give you, sir.
170 Hie you, make haste, for it grows very late.   *Exit.*
ROM: How well my comfort is reviv'd by this!
FRIAR: Go hence; good night; and here stands all your state:
Either be gone before the watch be set,
Or by the break of day disguis'd from hence.
175 Sojourn in Mantua. I'll find out your man,
And he shall signify from time to time
Every good hap to you that chances here.
Give me thy hand. 'Tis late. Farewell; good night.
ROM: But that a joy past joy calls out on me,
180 It were a grief so brief to part with thee.
Farewell.   *Exeunt.*

SCENE IV
Capulet's House

Enter Old Capulet, his Wife, and Paris.

CAP: Things have fall'n out, sir, so unluckily

[22]*persuade*

     That we have had no time to move[22] our daughter.

     Look you, she lov'd her kinsman Tybalt dearly,

     And so did I. Well, we were born to die.

5   'Tis very late; she'll not come down to-night.

     I promise you, but for your company,

     I would have been abed an hour ago.

PAR: These times of woe afford no tune to woo.

     Madam, good night. Commend me to your daughter.

10 LADY: I will, and know her mind early to-morrow;

[23]*shut up in her room*

     To-night she's mew'd up[23] to her heaviness.

CAP: Sir Paris, I will make a desperate tender

     Of my child's love. I think she will be rul'd

     In all respects by me; nay more, I doubt it not.

15   Wife, go you to her ere you go to bed;

     Acquaint her here of my son Paris' love

     And bid her (mark you me?) on Wednesday next—

     But, soft! what day is this?

PAR: Monday, my lord.

20 CAP: Monday! ha, ha! Well, Wednesday is too soon.

     Thursday let it be—a Thursday, tell her

     She shall be married to this noble earl.

     Will you be ready? Do you like this haste?

     We'll keep no great ado—a friend or two;

25   For hark you, Tybalt being slain so late,

     It may be thought we held him carelessly,

     Being our kinsman, if we revel much.

     Therefore we'll have some half a dozen friends,

     And there an end. But what say you to Thursday?

30 PAR: My lord, I would that Thursday were to-morrow.

CAP: Well, get you gone. A Thursday be it then.

     Go you to Juliet ere you go to bed;

     Prepare her, wife, against this wedding day.

     Farewell, my lord.—Light to my chamber, ho!

35   Afore me, it is so very very late

     That we may call it early by-and-by.

     Good night.   *Exeunt.*

SCENE V
Juliet's Chamber.

Enter Romeo and Juliet aloft, at the Window.

JUL: Wilt thou be gone? It is not yet near day.
It was the nightingale, and not the lark,
That pierc'd the fearful hollow of thine ear.
Nightly she sings on yon pomegranate tree.
5   Believe me, love, it was the nightingale.
ROM: It was the lark, the herald of the morn;
No nightingale. Look, love, what envious streaks
Do lace the severing clouds in yonder East.
Night's candles are burnt out, and jocund day
10   Stands tiptoe on the misty mountain tops.
I must be gone and live, or stay and die.
JUL: Yon light is not daylight; I know it, I.
It is some meteor that the sun exhales
To be to thee this night a torchbearer
15   And light thee on thy way to Mantua.
Therefore stay yet; thou need'st not to be gone.
ROM: Let me be ta'en, let me be put to death.
I am content, so thou wilt have it so.
I'll say yon grey is not the morning's eye,
20   'Tis but the pale reflex of Cynthia's[24] brow;
Nor that is not the lark whose notes do beat
The vaulty heaven so high above our heads.
I have more care to stay than will to go.
Come, death, and welcome! Juliet wills it so.
25   How is't, my soul? Let's talk; it is not day.
JUL: It is, it is! Hie hence, be gone, away!
It is the lark that sings so out of tune,
Straining harsh discords and unpleasing sharps.
Some say the lark makes sweet division;
30   This doth not so, for she divideth us.
Some say the lark and loathed toad changed eyes;
O, now I would they had chang'd voices too,
Since arm from arm that voice doth us affray,
Hunting thee hence with hunt's-up to the day!
35   O, now be gone! More light and light it grows.
ROM: More light and light—more dark and dark our woes!

[24]*the moon's*

Enter Nurse.

NURSE: Madam!
JUL: Nurse?
NURSE: Your lady mother is coming to your chamber.
40   The day is broke; be wary, look about.   *Exit Nurse.*
JUL: Then, window, let day in, and let life out.
ROM: Farewell, farewell! One kiss, and I'll descend.
                                        He goeth down.
JUL: Art thou gone so, my lord, my love, my friend?
      I must hear from thee every day in the hour,
45   For in a minute there are many days.
        O, by this count I shall be much in years
        Ere I again behold my Romeo!
ROM: Farewell! I will omit no opportunity
      That may convey my greetings, love, to thee.
50 JUL: O, think'st thou we shall ever meet again?
  ROM: I doubt it not; and all these woes shall serve
        For sweet discourses in our time to come.
JUL: O God, I have an ill-divining soul!
      Methinks I see thee, now thou art below,
55   As one dead in the bottom of a tomb.
        Either my eyesight fails, or thou look'st pale.
ROM: And trust me, love, in my eye so do you.
      Dry sorrow drinks our blood. Adieu, adieu!   *Exit.*
JUL: O Fortune, Fortune! all men call thee fickle.
60   If thou art fickle, what dost thou with him
        That is renown'd for faith? Be fickle, Fortune,
        For then I hope thou wilt not keep him long
        But send him back.
LADY: *Within.*   Ho, daughter! are you up?
65 JUL: Who is't that calls? It is my lady mother.
      Is she not down so late, or up so early?
      What unaccustom'd cause procures[25] her hither?

Enter Lady Capulet.

LADY: Why, how now, Juliet?
JUL: Madam, I am not well.
70 LADY: Evermore weeping for your cousin's death?

[25]brings

What, wilt thou wash him from his grave with tears?
An if thou could'st, thou could'st not make him live.
Therefore have done. Some grief shows much of love;
But much of grief shows still some want of wit.

75 JUL: Yet let me weep for such a feeling loss.

LADY: So shall you feel the loss, but not the friend
Which you weep for.

JUL: Feeling so the loss,
I cannot choose but ever weep the friend.

80 LADY: Well, girl, thou weep'st not so much for his death
As that the villain lives which slaughter'd him.

JUL: What villain, madam?

LADY: That same villain Romeo.

JUL: *Aside.* Villain and he be many miles asunder.[26]

[26]*apart*

85 God pardon him! I do, with all my heart;
And yet no man like he doth grieve my heart.

LADY: That is because the traitor murderer lives.

JUL: Ay, madam, from the reach of these my hands.
Would none but I might venge my cousin's death!

90 LADY: We will have vengeance for it, fear thou not.
Then weep no more. I'll send to one in Mantua,
Where that same banish'd runagate doth live,
Shall give him such an unaccustom'd dram[27]
That he shall soon keep Tybalt company;

[27]*dose of poison*

95 And then I hope thou wilt be satisfied.

JUL: Indeed I never shall be satisfied
With Romeo till I behold him—dead—
Is my poor heart so for a kinsman vex'd.
Madam, if you could find out but a man

100 To bear a poison, I would temper it;
That Romeo should, upon receipt thereof,
Soon sleep in quiet. O, how my heart abhors
To hear him nam'd and cannot come to him,
To wreak[28] the love I bore my cousin Tybalt

[28]*bear out*

105 Upon his body that hath slaughter'd him!

LADY: Find thou the means, and I'll find such a man.
But now I'll tell thee joyful tidings, girl.

JUL: And joy comes well in such a needy time.
What are they, I beseech your ladyship?

110 LADY: Well, well, thou hast a careful father, child;

One who, to put thee from thy heaviness,
Hath sorted out a sudden day of joy
That thou expects not, nor I look'd not for.
JUL: Madam, in happy time! What day is that?
115 LADY: Marry, my child, early next Thursday morn
The gallant, young, and noble gentleman,
The County Paris, at Saint Peter's Church,
Shall happily make thee there a joyful bride.
JUL: Now by Saint Peter's Church, and Peter too,
120   He shall not make me there a joyful bride!
I wonder at this haste, that I must wed
Ere he that should be husband comes to woo.
I pray you tell my lord and father, madam,
I will not marry yet; and when I do, I swear
125   It shall be Romeo, whom you know I hate,
Rather than Paris. These are news indeed!
LADY: Here comes your father. Tell him so yourself,
And see how he will take it at your hands.

Enter Capulet and Nurse.

CAP: When the sun sets the air doth drizzle dew,
130   But for the sunset of my brother's son
It rains downright.
How now? a conduit, girl? What, still in tears?
Evermore show'ring? In one little body
Thou counterfeit'st a bark,[29] a sea, a wind:
135   For still thy eyes, which I may call the sea,
Do ebb and flow with tears; the bark thy body is
Sailing in this salt flood; the winds, thy sighs,
Who, raging with thy tears and they with them,
Without a sudden calm will overset
140   Thy tempest-tossed body. How now, wife?
Have you delivered to her our decree?
LADY: Ay, sir; but she will none, she gives you thanks.
I would the fool were married to her grave!
CAP: Soft! take me with you, take me with you, wife.
145   How? Will she none? Doth she not give us thanks?
Is she not proud? Doth she not count her blest,
Unworthy as she is, that we have wrought
So worthy a gentleman to be her bridegroom?

[29]*ship*

JUL: Not proud you have, but thankful that you have.

150   Proud can I never be of what I hate,

But thankful even for hate that is meant love.

CAP: How, how, how, how, choplogic? What is this?

'Proud'—and 'I thank you'—and 'I thank you not'—

And yet 'not proud'? Mistress minion you,

155   Thank me no thankings, nor proud me no prouds,

But fettle[30] your fine joints 'gainst Thursday next

To go with Paris to Saint Peter's Church,

Or I will drag thee on a hurdle[31] thither.

Out, you green-sickness carrion! Out, you baggage!

160   You tallow-face!

LADY: Fie, fie! what, are you mad?

JUL: Good father, I beseech you on my knees,

Hear me with patience but to speak a word.

CAP: Hang thee, young baggage! disobedient wretch!

165   I tell thee what—get thee to church a Thursday

Or never after look me in the face.

Speak not, reply not, do not answer me!

My fingers itch. Wife, we scarce thought us blest

That God had lent us but this only child;

170   But now I see this one is one too much,

And that we have a curse in having her.

Out on her, hilding![32]

NURSE: God in heaven bless her!

You are to blame, my lord, to rate her so.

175 CAP: And why, my Lady Wisdom? Hold your tongue,

Good Prudence. Smatter with your gossips, go!

NURSE: I speak no treason.

CAP: O, God-i-god-en!

NURSE: May not one speak?

180 CAP: Peace, you mumbling fool!

Utter your gravity o'er a gossip's bowl,

For here we need it not.

LADY: You are too hot.

CAP: God's bread! It makes me mad.

185   Day, night, hour, tide, time, work, play,

Alone, in company, still my care hath been

To have her match'd; and having now provided

A gentleman of princely parentage,

Of fair demesnes,[33] youthful, and nobly train'd,

[30]*prepare*

[31]*sled used to transport convicts to execution*

[32]*worthless creature*

[33]*estates, property*

190   Stuff'd, as they say, with honourable parts,
        Proportion'd as one's thought would wish a man—
        And then to have a wretched puling[34] fool,
        A whining mammet, in her fortune's tender,
        To answer 'I'll not wed, I cannot love;
195   I am too young, I pray you pardon me'!
        But, an you will not wed, I'll pardon you.
        Graze where you will, you shall not house with me.
        Look to't, think on't; I do not use to jest.
        Thursday is near; lay hand on heart, advise:
200   An you be mine, I'll give you to my friend;
        An you be not, hang, beg, starve, die in the streets,
        For, by my soul, I'll ne'er acknowledge thee,
        Nor what is mine shall never do thee good.
        Trust to't. Bethink you. I'll not be forsworn.   *Exit.*
205 JUL: Is there no pity sitting in the clouds
        That sees into the bottom of my grief?
        O sweet my mother, cast me not away!
        Delay this marriage for a month, a week;
        Or if you do not, make the bridal bed
210   In that dim monument where Tybalt lies.
    LADY: Talk not to me, for I'll not speak a word.
        Do as thou wilt, for I have done with thee.   *Exit.*
    JUL: O God!—O nurse, how shall this be prevented?
        My husband is on earth, my faith in heaven.
215   How shall that faith return again to earth
        Unless that husband send it me from heaven
        By leaving earth? Comfort me, counsel me.
        Alack, alack, that heaven should practise stratagems
        Upon so soft a subject as myself!
220   What say'st thou? Hast thou not a word of joy?
        Some comfort, Nurse.
    NURSE: Faith, here it is.
        Romeo is banish'd; and all the world to nothing
        That he dares ne'er come back to challenge you;
225 ·   Or if he do, it needs must be by stealth.
        Then, since the case so stands as now it doth,
        I think it best you married with the County.
        O, he's a lovely gentleman!
        Romeo's a dishclout to him. An eagle, madam,

[34]whining

230   Hath not so green, so quick, so fair an eye
        As Paris hath. Beshrew my very heart,
        I think you are happy in this second match,
        For it excels your first; or if it did not,
        Your first is dead—or 'twere as good he were
235   As living here and you no use of him.
   JUL: Speak'st thou this from thy heart?
   NURSE: And from my soul too;
        Else beshrew them both.
   JUL: Amen!
240 NURSE: What?
   JUL: Well, thou hast comforted me marvellous much.
        Go in; and tell my lady I am gone,
        Having displeas'd my father, to Laurence' cell,
        To make confession and to be absolv'd.
245 NURSE: Marry, I will; and this is wisely done.   *Exit.*
   JUL: Ancient damnation! O most wicked fiend!
        Is it more sin to wish me thus forsworn,
        Or to dispraise my lord with that same tongue
        Which she hath prais'd him with above compare
250   So many thousand times? Go, counsellor!
        Thou and my bosom henceforth shall be twain.
        I'll to the friar to know his remedy.
        If all else fail, myself have power to die.   *Exit.*

ACT IV

SCENE I
Friar Laurence's cell.

Enter Friar Laurence and County Paris.

FRIAR: On Thursday, sir? The time is very short.
PAR: My father Capulet will have it so,
    And I am nothing slow to slack¹ his haste.
FRIAR: You say you do not know the lady's mind.
5   Uneven is the course; I like it not.
PAR: Immoderately she weeps for Tybalt's death,
    And therefore have I little talk'd of love;
    For Venus² smiles not in a house of tears.
    Now, sir, her father counts it dangerous
10   That she do give her sorrow so much sway,
    And in his wisdom hastes our marriage
    To stop the inundation of her tears,
    Which, too much minded by herself alone,
    May be put from her by society.
15   Now do you know the reason of this haste.
FRIAR: *Aside.* I would I knew not why it should be slow'd.
    Look, sir, here comes the lady toward my cell.

Enter Juliet.

PAR: Happily met, my lady and my wife!
JUL: That may be, sir, when I may be a wife.
20 **PAR:** That may be must be, love, on Thursday next.
JUL: What must be shall be.
FRIAR: That's a certain text.
PAR: Come you to make confession to this father?
JUL: To answer that, I should confess to you.

¹*quick to allow*

²*goddess of love*

³*value*

25 PAR: Do not deny to him that you love me.
    JUL: I will confess to you that I love him.
    PAR: So will ye, I am sure, that you love me.
    JUL: If I do so, it will be of more price,[3]
          Being spoke behind your back, than to your face.
30 PAR: Poor soul, thy face is much abus'd with tears.
    JUL: The tears have got small victory by that,
          For it was bad enough before their spite.
    PAR: Thou wrong'st it more than tears with that report.
    JUL: That is no slander, sir, which is a truth;
35   And what I spake, I spake it to my face.
    PAR: Thy face is mine, and thou hast sland'red it.
    JUL: It may be so, for it is not mine own.
          Are you at leisure, holy father, now,
          Or shall I come to you at evening mass?
40 FRIAR: My leisure serves me, pensive daughter, now.
          My lord, we must entreat the time alone.
    PAR: God shield I should disturb devotion!
          Juliet, on Thursday early will I rouse ye.
          Till then, adieu, and keep this holy kiss.   *Exit.*
45 JUL: O, shut the door! and when thou hast done so,
          Come weep with me—past hope, past cure, past help!
    FRIAR: Ah, Juliet, I already know thy grief;
          It strains me past the compass of my wits.
          I hear thou must, and nothing may prorogue[4] it,
50   On Thursday next be married to this County.
    JUL: Tell me not, friar, that thou hear'st of this,
          Unless thou tell me how I may prevent it.
          If in thy wisdom thou canst give no help,
          Do thou but call my resolution wise
55   And with this knife I'll help it presently.
          God join'd my heart and Romeo's, thou our hands;
          And ere this hand, by thee to Romeo seal'd,
          Shall be the label to another deed,
          Or my true heart with treacherous revolt
60   Turn to another, this shall slay them both.
          Therefore, out of thy long-experienc'd time,
          Give me some present counsel; or, behold,
          'Twixt my extremes and me this bloody knife
          Shall play the umpire, arbitrating that
65   Which the commission of thy years and art

⁴*defer, delay*

Could to no issue of true honour bring.
Be not so long to speak. I long to die
If what thou speak'st speak not of remedy.
FRIAR: Hold, daughter. I do spy a kind of hope,
70   Which craves[5] as desperate an execution
As that is desperate which we would prevent.
If, rather than to marry County Paris,
Thou hast the strength of will to slay thyself,
Then is it likely thou wilt undertake
75   A thing like death to chide[6] away this shame,
That cop'st[7] with death himself to scape from it;
And, if thou dar'st, I'll give thee remedy.
JUL: O, bid me leap, rather than marry Paris,
From off the battlements of yonder tower,
80   Or walk in thievish ways, or bid me lurk
Where serpents are; chain me with roaring bears,
Or shut me nightly in a charnel house,
O'ercover'd quite with dead men's rattling bones,
With reeky shanks and yellow chapless skulls;
85   Or bid me go into a new-made grave
And hide me with a dead man in his shroud—
Things that, to hear them told, have made me tremble—
And I will do it without fear or doubt,
To live an unstain'd wife to my sweet love.
90 FRIAR: Hold, then. Go home, be merry, give consent
To marry Paris. Wednesday is to-morrow.
To-morrow night look that thou lie alone;
Let not the nurse lie with thee in thy chamber.
Take thou this vial, being then in bed,
95   And this distilled liquor drink thou off;
When presently through all thy veins shall run
A cold and drowsy humour; for no pulse
Shall keep his native progress, but surcease;
No warmth, no breath, shall testify thou liv'st;
100   The roses in thy lips and cheeks shall fade
To paly ashes, thy eyes' windows fall
Like death when he shuts up the day of life;
Each part, depriv'd of supple government,
Shall, stiff and stark and cold, appear like death;
105   And in this borrowed likeness of shrunk death
Thou shalt continue two-and-forty hours,

[5]*demands*

[6]*rebuke, force*

[7]*struggles*

And then awake as from a pleasant sleep.
Now, when the bridegroom in the morning comes
To rouse thee from thy bed, there art thou dead.
110 Then, as the manner of our country is,
In thy best robes uncovered on the bier
Thou shalt be borne to that same ancient vault
Where all the kindred of the Capulets lie.
In the mean time, against thou shalt awake,

[8]plan

115 Shall Romeo by my letters know our drift;[8]
And hither shall he come; and he and I
Will watch thy waking, and that very night
Shall Romeo bear thee hence to Mantua.
And this shall free thee from this present shame,
120 If no inconstant toy nor womanish fear
Abate thy valour in the acting it.
JUL: Give me, give me! O, tell not me of fear!
FRIAR: Hold! Get you gone, be strong and prosperous
In this resolve. I'll send a friar with speed
125 To Mantua, with my letters to thy lord.
JUL: Love give me strength! and strength shall help afford.
Farewell, dear father.

Exeunt.

SCENE II
Capulet's House.

*Enter Father Capulet, Lady Capulet, Nurse, and Servingmen,
two or three.*

CAP: So many guests invite as here are writ.

Exit a Servingman.

[9]skillful

Sirrah, go hire me twenty cunning[9] cooks.
SERV: You shall have none ill, sir; for I'll try if they can lick
their fingers.
5 CAP: How canst thou try them so?
SERV: Marry, sir, 'tis an ill cook that cannot lick his own
fingers. Therefore he that cannot lick his fingers goes
not with me.

CAP: Go, begone.   *Exit Servingman.*

10   We shall be much unfurnish'd[10] for this time.
          What, is my daughter gone to Friar Laurence?
NURSE: Ay, forsooth.
CAP: Well, be may chance to do some good on her.
          A peevish self-will'd harlotry it is.

Enter Juliet.

15 NURSE: See where she comes from shrift with merry look.
CAP: How now, my headstrong? Where have you been
          gadding?
JUL: Where I have learnt me to repent the sin
          Of disobedient opposition
20   To you and your behests, and am enjoin'd
          By holy Laurence to fall prostrate here
          To beg your pardon. Pardon, I beseech you!
          Henceforward I am ever rul'd by you.
CAP: Send for the County. Go tell him of this.
25   I'll have this knot knit up to-morrow morning.
JUL: I met the youthful lord at Laurence' cell
          And gave him what becomed[11] love I might,
          Not stepping o'er the bounds of modesty.
CAP: Why, I am glad on't. This is well. Stand up.
30   This is as't should be. Let me see the County.
          Ay, marry, go, I say, and fetch him hither.
          Now, afore God, this reverend holy friar,
          All our whole city is much bound to him.
JUL: Nurse, will you go with me into my closet
35   To help me sort such needful ornaments
          As you think fit to furnish me to-morrow?
LADY CAP: No, not till Thursday. There is time enough.
CAP: Go, nurse, go with her. We'll to church to-morrow.
                              Exeunt Juliet and Nurse.
LADY CAP: We shall be short in our provision.
40   'Tis now near night.
CAP: Tush, I will stir about,
          And all things shall be well, I warrant thee, wife.
          Go thou to Juliet, help to deck up her.
          I'll not to bed to-night; let me alone.

[10]*unprepared*

[11]*fitting, appropriate*

45   I'll play the housewife for this once. What, ho!
        They are all forth; well, I will walk myself
        To County Paris, to prepare him up
        Against to-morrow. My heart is wondrous light,
        Since this same wayward girl is so reclaim'd.

                                              Exeunt.

SCENE III
Juliet's Chamber.

Enter Juliet and Nurse.

JUL: Ay, those attires are best; but, gentle nurse,
        I pray thee leave me to myself to-night;
        For I have need of many orisons[12]
        To move the heavens to smile upon my state,
5   Which, well thou knowest, is cross and full of sin.

Enter Lady Cap.

LADY CAP: What, are you busy, ho? Need you my help?
JUL: No, madam; we have cull'd[13] such necessaries
        As are behoveful for our state to-morrow.
        So please you, let me now be left alone,
10   And let the nurse this night sit up with you;
        For I am sure you have your hands full all
        In this so sudden business.
LADY CAP: Good night.
        Get thee to bed, and rest; for thou hast need.
                            Exeunt Lady Capulet and Nurse.
15 JUL: Farewell! God knows when we shall meet again.
        I have a faint cold fear thrills through my veins
        That almost freezes up the heat of life.
        I'll call them back again to comfort me.
        Nurse!—What should she do here?
20   My dismal scene I needs must act alone.
        Come, vial.
        What if this mixture do not work at all?

[12]*prayers*

[13]*gathered, collected*

Shall I be married then to-morrow morning?
No, No! This shall forbid it. Lie thou there.
Lays down a dagger.
25   What if it be a poison which the friar
Subtly hath ministr'd to have me dead,
Lest in this marriage he should be dishonour'd
Because he married me before to Romeo?
I fear it is; and yet methinks it should not,
30   For he hath still been tried a holy man.
I will not entertain so bad a thought.
How if, when I am laid into the tomb,
I wake before the time that Romeo
Come to redeem me? There's a fearful point!
35   Shall I not then be stifled in the vault,
To whose foul mouth no healthsome air breathes in,
And there die strangled ere my Romeo comes?
Or, if I live, is it not very like
The horrible conceit of death and night,
40   Together with the terror of the place—
As in a vault, an ancient receptacle
Where for this many hundred years the bones
Of all my buried ancestors are pack'd;
Where bloody Tybalt, yet but green in earth,
45   Lies fest'ring in his shroud; where, as they say,
At some hours in the night spirits resort—
Alack, alack, is it not like that I,
So early waking—what with loathsome smells,
And shrieks like mandrakes torn out of the earth,
50   That living mortals, hearing them, run mad—
O, if I wake, shall I not be distraught,
Environed with all these hideous fears,
And madly play with my forefathers' joints,
And pluck the mangled Tybalt from his shroud,
55   And, in this rage, with some great kinsman's bone
As with a club dash out my desp'rate brains?
O, look! methinks I see my cousin's ghost
Seeking out Romeo, that did spit[14] his body
Upon a rapier's point. Stay, Tybalt, stay!
60   Romeo, I come! this do I drink to thee.
She drinks and falls upon her bed within the curtains.

[14]skewer

SCENE IV
Capulet's House.

Enter Lady Capulet and Nurse.

LADY: Hold, take these keys and fetch more spices, Nurse.
NURSE: They call for dates and quinces in the pastry.

Enter Capulet.

CAP: Come, stir, stir, stir! The second cock hath crow'd,
    The curfew bell hath rung, 'tis three o'clock.
5   ·Look to the bak'd meats, good Angelica;
    Spare not for cost.
NURSE: Go, you cot-quean,[15] go,
    Get you to bed! Faith, you'll be sick to-morrow
    For this night's watching.[16]
10 CAP: No, not a whit. What, I have watch'd ere now
    All night for lesser cause, and ne'er been sick.
LADY: Ay, you have been a mouse-hunt[17] in your time;
    But I will watch you from such watching now.
                      Exeunt Lady and Nurse.
CAP: A jealous hood, a jealous hood![18]
15   Now, fellow, what is there?

Enter three or four servingmen, with spits and logs and baskets.

FIRST SERVANT: Things for the cook, sir; but I know not
    what.
CAP: Make haste, make haste. *Exit First Servant.* Sirrah,
    fetch drier logs.
20   Call Peter; he will show thee where they are.
SECOND SERVANT: I have a head, sir, that will find out logs
    And never trouble Peter for the matter.
                      Exit Second Servant.
CAP: Mass, and well said; a merry whoreson, ha!
    Thou shalt be loggerhead.Good faith,'tis day.
25   The County will be here with music straight,
    For so he said he would.   *Play of music.*

[15]*husband who does wife's household work*

[16]*staying awake*

[17]*woman chaser*

[18]*i.e., you wear the hood of jealousy*

I hear him near.
Nurse! Wife! What, ho! What, nurse, I say!
Enter Nurse.
Go waken Juliet; go and trim her up.
30 I'll go and chat with Paris. Hie, make haste,
Make haste! The bridegroom he is come already:
Make haste, I say.

Exeunt.

SCENE V
Juliet's Chamber.

Enter Nurse.

NURSE: Mistress! what, mistress! Juliet! Fast,[19] I warrant
        her, she.
    Why, lamb! why, lady! Fie, you slug-abed!
    Why, love, I say! madam! sweetheart! Why, bride!
5   What, not a word? You take your pennyworths[20] now!
    Sleep for a week; for the next night, I warrant,
    The County Paris hath set up his rest
    That you shall rest but little. God forgive me!
    Marry, and amen. How sound is she asleep!
10 I needs must wake her. Madam, madam, madam!
    Ay, let the County take you in your bed!
    He'll fright you up, i' faith. Will it not be?
Draws aside the curtains.
    What, dress'd, and in your clothes, and down again?
    I must needs wake you. Lady! lady! lady!
15 Alas, alas! Help, help! My lady's dead!
    O well-a-day that ever I was born!
    Some aqua-vitae, ho! My lord! my lady!

Enter Lady Capulet.

LADY CAP: What noise is here?
NURSE: O lamentable day!
20 LADY CAP: What is the matter?

[19] *fast asleep*

[20] *of sleep*

NURSE: Look, look! O heavy day!
LADY CAP: O me, O me! My child, my only life!
    Revive, look up, or I will die with thee!
    Help, help! Call help.

Enter Capulet.

25 CAP: For shame, bring Juliet forth; her lord is come.
    NURSE: She's dead, deceas'd; she's dead! Alack the day!
    LADY CAP: Alack the day, she's dead, she's dead, she's dead!
    CAP: Ha! let me see her. Out alas! she's cold,
    Her blood is settled, and her joints are stiff;
30 Life and these lips have long been separated.
    Death lies on her like an untimely frost
    Upon the sweetest flower of all the field.
    NURSE: O lamentable day!
    LADY CAP: O woful time!
35 CAP: Death, that hath ta'en her hence to make me wail,
    Ties up my tongue and will not let me speak.

Enter Friar Laurence and the County (Paris), with Musicians.

FRIAR: Come, is the bride ready to go to church?
CAP: Ready to go, but never to return.
    O son, the night before thy wedding day
    Hath Death lain with thy wife. See, there she lies,
40 Flower as she was, deflowered by him.
    Death is my son-in-law, Death is my heir;
    My daughter he hath wedded. I will die
    And leave him all. Life, living, all is Death's.
PAR: Have I thought long to see this morning's face,
45 And doth it give me such a sight as this?
    LADY CAPULET: Accurs'd, unhappy, wretched, hateful day!
    Most miserable hour that e'er time saw
    In lasting labour of his pilgrimage!
    But one, poor one, one poor and loving child,
50 But one thing to rejoice and solace in,
    And cruel Death hath catch'd it from my sight!
    NURSE: O woe! O woeful, woeful, woeful day!
    Most lamentable day, most woeful day

That ever ever I did yet behold!
55 O day! O day! O day! O hateful day!
Never was seen so black a day as this.
O woeful day! O woeful day!

PAR: Beguil'd,[21] divorced, wronged, spited, slain!
Most detestable Death, by thee beguil'd,
60 By cruel cruel thee quite overthrown!
O love! O life! not life, but love in death!

CAP: Despis'd, distressed, hated, martyr'd, kill'd!
Uncomfortable time, why cam'st thou now
To murder, murder our solemnity?[22]
65 O child! O child! my soul, and not my child!
Dead art thou, dead! alack, my child is dead,
And with my child my joys are buried!

FRIAR: Peace, ho, for shame! Confusion's cure lives not
In these confusions. Heaven and yourself
70 Had part in this fair maid! now heaven hath all,
And all the better is it for the maid.
Your part in her you could not keep from death,
But heaven keeps his part in eternal life.
The most you sought was her promotion,
75 For 'twas your heaven she should be advanc'd;
And weep ye now, seeing she is advanc'd
Above the clouds, as high as heaven itself?
O, in this love, you love your child so ill
That you run mad, seeing that she is well.
80 She's not well married that lives married long,
But she's best married that dies married young.
Dry up your tears and stick your rosemary[23]
On this fair corse, and, as the custom is,
In all her best array bear her to church;
85 For though fond nature bids us all lament,
Yet nature's tears are reason's merriment.[24]

CAP: All things that we ordained festival[25]
Turn from their office to black funeral—
Our instruments to melancholy bells,
90 Our wedding cheer to a sad burial feast;
Our solemn hymns to sullen dirges change;
Our bridal flowers serve for a buried corse;
And all things change them to the contrary.

[21]*cheated*

[22]*festivities*

[23]*fragrant evergreen*

[24]*i.e., reason laughs at sorrow*

[25]*for celebration*

FRIAR: Sir, go you in; and, madam, go with him;
95   And go, Sir Paris. Every one prepare
        To follow this fair corse unto her grave.
        The heavens do low'r upon you for some ill;
        Move them no more by crossing their high will.
                Exeunt. Capulet, Lady Capulet, Paris,and Friar.
        1. MUS: Faith, we may put up our pipes and be gone.
100 NURSE: Honest good fellows, ah, put up, put up!
        For well you know this is a pitiful case.
                                        Exit Nurse.
        1. MUS: Ay, by my troth, the case may be amended.

Enter Peter.

        PET: Musicians, O, musicians, 'Heart's ease, Heart's ease'!
        O, an you will have me live, play 'Heart's ease.'
105 1. MUS: Why 'Heart's ease'?
        PET: O, musicians, because my heart itself plays 'My heart is full
                of woe.' O, play me some merry dump to comfort me.
        1. MUS: Not a dump we! 'Tis no time to play now.
        PET: You will not then?
110 1. MUS: No.
        PET: I will then give it you soundly.
        1. MUS: What will you give us?
        PET: No money, on my faith, but the gleek.[26] I will give[27]
                you the minstrel.
115 1. MUS: Then will I give you the serving-creature.
        PET: Then will I lay the serving-creature's dagger on your
                pate. I will carry no crotchets. I'll re you, I'll fa you. Do
                you note me?
        1. MUS: An you re us and fa us, you note us.
120 2. MUS: Pray you put up your dagger, and put out your
                wit.
        PET: Then have at you with my wit! I will dry-beat you
                with an iron wit, and put up my iron dagger. Answer
                me like men.
125   'When griping grief the heart doth wound,
                And doleful dumps the mind oppress,
                Then music with her silver sound'—
        Why 'silver sound'? Why 'music with her silver sound'?

[26]*scorn*

[27]*call*

What say you, Simon Catling?

130 **1. Mus:** Marry, sir, because silver hath a sweet sound.

Pet: Pretty! What say you, Hugh Rebeck?

2. Mus: I say 'silver sound' because musicians sound for silver.

Pet: Pretty too! What say you, James Soundpost?

135 **3. Mus:** Faith, I know not what to say.

Pet: O, I cry you mercy! you are the singer. I will say for you. It is 'music with her silver sound' because musicians have no gold for sounding.

'Then music with her silver sound

140   With speedy help doth lend redress.'   *Exit.*

1. Mus: What a pestilent knave is this same!

2. Mus: Hang him, Jack! Come, we'll in here, tarry for the mourners, and stay dinner.

                                Exeunt.

ACT V

SCENE I
Mantua. A street.

Enter Romeo.

ROM: If I may trust the flattering truth of sleep,
My dreams presage[1] some joyful news at hand.
My bosom's lord sits lightly in his throne,
And all this day an unaccustom'd spirit
5 Lifts me above the ground with cheerful thoughts.
I dreamt my lady came and found me dead
(Strange dream that gives a dead man leave to think!)
And breath'd such life with kisses in my lips
That I reviv'd and was an emperor.
10 Ah me! how sweet is love itself possess'd,
When but love's shadows are so rich in joy!

Enter Romeo's man Balthasar, booted.

News from Verona! How now, Balthasar?
Dost thou not bring me letters from the friar?
How doth my lady? Is my father well?
15 How fares my Juliet? That I ask again,
For nothing can be ill if she be well.

MAN: Then she is well, and nothing can be ill.
Her body sleeps in Capels' monument,
And her immortal part with angels lives.
20 I saw her laid low in her kindred's vault
And presently took post to tell it you.
O, pardon me for bringing these ill news,
Since you did leave it for my office, sir.

ROM: Is it e'en so? Then I defy you, stars!
25 Thou knowest my lodging. Get me ink and paper
And hire posthorses. I will hence to-night.

[1]*predict*

MAN: I do beseech you, sir, have patience.

      Your looks are pale and wild and do import²

      Some misadventure.

30 ROM: Tush, thou art deceiv'd.

      Leave me and do the thing I bid thee do.

      Hast thou no letters to me from the friar?

MAN: No, my good lord.

ROM: No matter. Get thee gone

35   And hire those horses. I'll be with thee straight.

                       Exit Balthasar.

      Well, Juliet, I will lie with thee to-night.

      Let's see for means. O mischief, thou art swift

      To enter in the thoughts of desperate men!

      I do remember an apothecary,³

40   And hereabouts he dwells, which late I noted

      In tatt'red weeds, with overwhelming brows,

      Culling of simples.⁴ Meagre were his looks,

      Sharp misery had worn him to the bones;

      And in his needy shop a tortoise hung,

45   An alligator stuff'd, and other skins

      Of ill-shaped fishes; and about his shelves

      A beggarly account of empty boxes,

      Green earthen pots, bladders, and musty seeds,

      Remnants of packthread, and old cakes of roses

50   Were thinly scattered, to make up a show.

      Noting this penury, to myself I said,

      'An if a man did need a poison now

      Whose sale is present death in Mantua,

      Here lives a caitiff⁵ wretch would sell it him.'

55   O, this same thought did but forerun my need,

      And this same needy man must sell it me.

      As I remember, this should be the house.

      Being holiday, the beggar's shop is shut.

      What, ho! apothecary!

Enter Apothecary.

60 APOTH: Who calls so loud?

ROM: Come hither, man. I see that thou art poor.

      Hold, there is forty ducats. Let me have

A dram of poison, such soon-speeding gear
As will disperse itself through all the veins

65 That the life-weary taker may fall dead,
And that the trunk may be discharg'd of breath
As violently as hasty powder fir'd
Doth hurry from the fatal cannon's womb.

APOTH: Such mortal drugs I have; but Mantua's law
70 Is death to any he that utters them.

ROM: Art thou so bare and full of wretchedness
And fearest to die? Famine is in thy cheeks,
Need and oppression starveth in thine eyes,
Contempt and beggary hangs upon thy back:

75 The world is not thy friend, nor the world's law;
The world affords no law to make thee rich;
Then be not poor, but break it and take this.

APOTH: My poverty but not my will consents.

ROM: I pay thy poverty and not thy will.

80 APOTH: Put this in any liquid thing you will
And drink it off, and if you had the strength
Of twenty men, it would dispatch you straight.

ROM: There is thy gold—worse poison to men's souls,
Doing more murderer in this loathsome world,

85 Than these poor compounds that thou mayst not sell.
I sell thee poison; thou hast sold me none.
Farewell. Buy food and get thyself in flesh.
Come, cordial and not poison, go with me
To Juliet's grave; for there must I use thee.

              Exeunt.

SCENE II
Verona. Friar Laurence's Cell.

Enter Friar John.

JOHN: Holy Franciscan friar, brother, ho!

Enter Friar Laurence.

LAUR: This same should be the voice of Friar John.
    Welcome from Mantua. What says Romeo?
    Or, if his mind be writ, give me his letter.
5 JOHN: Going to find a barefoot brother out,
    One of our order, to associate[6] me
    Here in this city visiting the sick,
    And finding him, the searchers of the town,
    Suspecting that we both were in a house
10   Where the infectious pestilence did reign,
    Seal'd up the doors, and would not let us forth,
    So that my speed to Mantua there was stay'd.
LAUR: Who bare my letter, then, to Romeo?
JOHN: I could not send it—here it is again—
15   Nor get a messenger to bring it thee,
    So fearful were they of infection.
LAUR: Unhappy fortune! By my brotherhood,
    The letter was not nice,[7] but full of charge,
    Of dear import;[8] and the neglecting it
20   May do much danger. Friar John, go hence,
    Get me an iron crow and bring it straight
    Unto my cell.
JOHN: Brother, I'll go and bring it thee.   *Exit.*
LAUR: Now, must I to the monument alone.
25   Within this three hours will fair Juliet wake.
    She will beshrew[9] me much that Romeo
    Hath had no notice of these accidents;
    But I will write again to Mantua,
    And keep her at my cell till Romeo come—
30   Poor living corse, clos'd in a dead man's tomb! *Exit.*

[6]*assist*

[7]*trivial*

[8]*grave importance*

[9]*criticize*

SCENE III
Verona. A Churchyard; in it, the monument of the Capulets.

Enter Paris and his Page with flowers and a torch.

PAR: Give me thy torch, boy. Hence, and stand aloof.
Yet put it[10] out, for I would not be seen.
Under yond yew tree lay thee all along,
Holding thine ear close to the hollow ground.

5   So shall no foot upon the churchyard tread
(Being loose, unfirm, with digging up of graves)
But thou shalt hear it. Whistle then to me,
As signal that thou hear'st something approach.
Give me those flowers. Do as I bid thee, go.

10 PAGE: *Aside.*   I am almost afraid to stand alone
Here in the churchyard; yet I will adventure.   *Retires.*
PAR: Sweet flower, with flowers thy bridal bed I strew
(O woe! thy canopy is dust and stones)
Which with sweet water nightly I will dew;

15   Or, wanting that, with tears distill'd by moans.
The obsequies[11] that I for thee will keep
Nightly shall be to strew thy grave and weep.
The Page whistles.
The boy gives warning something doth approach.
What cursed foot wanders this way to-night

20   To cross my obsequies and true love's rite?
What, with a torch? Muffle me, night, a while.   *Retires.*

Enter Romeo and Balthasar with a torch, a mattock, and a crow[12] of iron.

ROM: Give me that mattock and the wrenching iron.
Hold, take this letter. Early in the morning
See thou deliver it to my lord and father.

25   Give me the light. Upon thy life I charge thee,
Whate'er thou hearest or seest, stand all aloof
And do not interrupt me in my course.
Why I descend into this bed of death
Is partly to behold my lady's face,

30   But chiefly to take thence from her dead finger

[10]*the torch*

[11]*funeral rites*

[12]*a crowbar*

A precious ring—a ring that I must use
In dear employment. Therefore hence, be gone.
But if thou, jealous, dost return to pry
In what I further shall intend to do,

35   By heaven, I will tear thee joint by joint
And strew this hungry churchyard with thy limbs.
The time and my intents are savage-wild,

[13]*unstoppable*

More fierce and more inexorable[13] far
Than empty tigers or the roaring sea.

40 BAL: I will be gone, sir, and not trouble you.
    ROM: So shalt thou show me friendship. Take thou that.
    Live, and be prosperous; and farewell, good fellow.
    BAL: *Aside.* For all this same, I'll hide me hereabout.
    His looks I fear, and his intents I doubt.   *Retires.*

[14]*mouth*

45 ROM: Thou detestable maw,[14] thou womb of death,
    Gorg'd with the dearest morsel of the earth,
    Thus I enforce thy rotten jaws to open,
    And in despite I'll cram thee with more food.

Romeo opens the tomb.

    PAR: This is that banish'd haughty Montague
50   That murdered my love's cousin—with which grief
    It is supposed the fair creature died—
    And here is come to do some villanous shame
    To the dead bodies. I will apprehend him.
    Stop thy unhallowed toil, vile Montague!
55   Can vengeance be pursu'd further than death?
    Condemned villain, I do apprehend thee.
    Obey, and go with me; for thou must die.
    ROM: I must indeed; and therefore came I hither.
    Good gentle youth, tempt not a desp'rate man.
60   Fly hence and leave me. Think upon these gone;
    Let them affright thee. I beseech thee, youth,
    Put not another sin upon my head
    By urging me to fury. O, be gone!
    By heaven, I love thee better than myself,
65   For I come hither arm'd against myself.
    Stay not, be gone. Live, and hereafter say
    A madman's mercy bid thee run away.

PAR: I do defy thy conjuration[15]

    And apprehend thee for a felon here.

70 ROM: Wilt thou provoke me? Then have at thee, boy!

                         They fight.

PAGE: O Lord, they fight! I will go call the watch.

                  Exit. Paris falls.

PAR: O, I am slain! If thou be merciful,

    Open the tomb, lay me with Juliet.   *Dies.*

ROM: In faith, I will. Let me peruse this face.

75   Mercutio's kinsman, noble County Paris!

    What said my man when my betossed soul

    Did not attend him as we rode? I think

    He told me Paris should have married Juliet.

    Said he not so? or did I dream it so?

80   Or am I mad, hearing him talk of Juliet

    To think it was so? O, give me thy hand,

    One writ with me in sour misfortune's book!

    I'll bury thee in a triumphant grave.

    A grave? O, no, a lantern, slaughtr'd youth,

85   For here lies Juliet, and her beauty makes

    This vault a feasting presence full of light.

    Death, lie thou there, by a dead man interr'd.

Lays him in the tomb.

    How oft when men are at the point of death

    Have they been merry! which their keepers call

90   A lightning before death. O, how may I

    Call this a lightning? O my love! my wife!

    Death, that hath suck'd the honey of thy breath,

    Hath had no power yet upon thy beauty.

    Thou art not conquer'd. Beauty's ensign[16] yet

95   Is crimson in thy lips and in thy cheeks,

    And death's pale flag is not advanced there.

    Tybalt, liest thou there in thy bloody sheet?

    O, what more favour can I do to thee

    Than with that hand that cut thy youth in twain

100   To sunder his that was thine enemy?

    Forgive me, cousin. Ah, dear Juliet,

    Why art thou yet so fair? Shall I believe

    That unsubstantial Death is amorous,

    And that the lean abhorred monster keeps

[15]*demand*

[16]*sign, banner*

105   Thee here in dark to be his paramour?
For fear of that I still will stay with thee
And never from this palace of dim night
Depart again. Here, here will I remain
With worms that are thy chambermaids. O, here
110   Will I set up my everlasting rest
And shake the yoke of inauspicious[17] stars
From this world-wearied flesh. Eyes, look your last!
Arms, take your last embrace! and, lips, O you
The doors of breath, seal with a righteous kiss
115   A dateless bargain to engrossing death!
Come, bitter conduct; come, unsavoury guide!
Thou desperate pilot, now at once run on
The dashing rocks thy seasick weary bark!
Here's to my love!   *Drinks.*   O true apothecary!
120   Thy drugs are quick. Thus with a kiss I die.   *Falls.*

Enter Friar Laurence, with lantern, crow, and spade.

FRIAR: Saint Francis be my speed! how oft to-night
      Have my old feet stumbled at graves! Who's there?
BAL: Here's one, a friend, and one that knows you well.
FRIAR: Bliss be upon you! Tell me, good my friend,
125   What torch is yond that vainly lends his light
      To grubs and eyeless skulls? As I discern,
      It burneth in the Capels' monument.
BAL: It doth so, holy sir; and there's my master,
      One that you love.
130   FRIAR: Who is it?
BAL: Romeo.
FRIAR: How long hath he been there?
BAL: Full half an hour.
FRIAR: Go with me to the vault.
135   BAL: I dare not, sir.
      My master knows not but I am gone hence,
      And fearfully did menace me with death
      If I did stay to look on his intents.
FRIAR: Stay then; I'll go alone. Fear comes upon me.
140   O, much I fear some ill unlucky thing.
BAL: As I did sleep under this yew tree here,

[17]*unhappy*

I dreamt my master and another fought,
And that my master slew him.
FRIAR: Romeo!
145   Alack, alack, what blood is this which stains
The stony entrance of this sepulchre?
What mean these masterless and gory swords
To lie discolour'd by this place of peace?

                         Enters the tomb.

Romeo! O, pale! Who else? What, Paris too?
150   And steep'd in blood? Ah, what an unkind hour
Is guilty of this lamentable chance!
The lady stirs.   *Juliet rises.*
JUL: O comfortable friar! where is my lord?
I do remember well where I should be,
155   And there I am. Where is my Romeo?
FRIAR: I hear some noise. Lady, come from that nest
Of death, contagion, and unnatural sleep.
A greater power than we can contradict
Hath thwarted our intents. Come, come away.
160   Thy husband in thy bosom there lies dead;
And Paris too. Come, I'll dispose of thee
Among a sisterhood of holy nuns.
Stay not to question, for the watch is coming.
Come, go, good Juliet. I dare no longer stay.
165 JUL: Go, get thee hence, for I will not away.

                         Exit Friar.

What's here? A cup, clos'd in my true love's hand?
Poison, I see, hath been his timeless end.
O churl! drunk all, and left no friendly drop
To help me after? I will kiss thy lips.
170   Haply some poison yet doth hang on them
To make me die with a restorative.   *Kisses him.*
Thy lips are warm!
CHIEF WATCH: *Within.*   Lead, boy. Which way?
JUL: Yea, noise? Then I'll be brief. O happy dagger!

                     Snatches Romeo's dagger.

175   This is thy sheath; there rust, and let me die.

                She stabs herself and falls on Romeo's body.

Enter Paris' Boy and Watch.

BOY: This is the place. There, where the torch doth burn.
180 CHIEF WATCH: The ground is bloody. Search about the
                churchyard.
        Go, some of you; whoe'er you find attach.
                                    Exeunt some of the Watch.
        Pitiful sight! here lies the County slain;
        And Juliet bleeding, warm, and newly dead,
185   Who here hath lain this two days buried.
        Go, tell the Prince; run to the Capulets;
        Raise up the Montagues; some others search.
                                    Exeunt others of the Watch.
        We see the ground whereon these woes do lie,
        But the true ground of all these piteous woes
190   We cannot without circumstance descry.[18]

Enter some of the Watch, with Romeo's Man Balthasar.

2. WATCH: Here's Romeo's man. We found him in the
        churchyard.
CHIEF WATCH: Hold him in safety till the Prince come
        hither.

Enter Friar Laurence and another Watchman.

195 3. WATCH: Here is a friar that trembles, sighs, and weeps.
        We took this mattock and this spade from him
        As he was coming from this churchyard side.
CHIEF WATCH: A great suspicion! Stay the friar too.

Enter the Prince and Attendants.

PRINCE: What misadventure is so early up,
200   That calls our person from our morning rest?

Enter Capulet, Lady Capulet, and others.

CAP: What should it be, that they so shriek abroad?
LADY CAPULET: The people in the street cry 'Romeo,'
        Some 'Juliet,' and some 'Paris'; and all run,
        With open outcry, toward our monument.

[18]*figure out, decipher*

205 PRINCE: What fear is this which startles in our ears?
       CHIEF WATCH: Sovereign, here lies the County Paris slain;
             And Romeo dead; and Juliet, dead before,
             Warm and new kill'd.
       PRINCE: Search, seek, and know how this foul murder comes.
210 CHIEF WATCH: Here is a friar, and slaughter'd Romeo's man,
             With instruments upon them fit to open
             These dead men's tombs.
       CAP: O heavens! O wife, look how our daughter bleeds!
             This dagger hath mista'en, for, lo, his house[19]
215   Is empty on the back of Montague,
             And it missheathed in my daughter's bosom!
       LADY CAPULET: O me! this sight of death is as a bell
             That warns my old age to a sepulchre.

Enter Montague and others.

       PRINCE: Come, Montague; for thou art early up
220   To see thy son and heir more early down.
       MON: Alas, my liege, my wife is dead to-night!
             Grief of my son's exile hath stopp'd her breath.
             What further woe conspires against mine age?
       PRINCE: Look, and thou shalt see.
225 MON: O thou untaught! what manners is in this,
             To press before thy father to a grave?
       PRINCE: Seal up the mouth of outrage for a while,
             Till we can clear these ambiguities
             And know their spring, their head, their true descent;
230   And then will I be general of your woes
             And lead you even to death. Meantime forbear,
             And let mischance be slave to patience.
             Bring forth the parties of suspicion.
       FRIAR: I am the greatest, able to do least,
235   Yet most suspected, as the time and place
             Doth make against me, of this direful murder;
             And here I stand, both to impeach and purge
             Myself condemned and myself excus'd.
       PRINCE: Then say at once what thou dost know in this.
240 FRIAR: I will be brief, for my short date of breath
             Is not so long as is a tedious tale.

[19]*the dagger's empty scabbard*

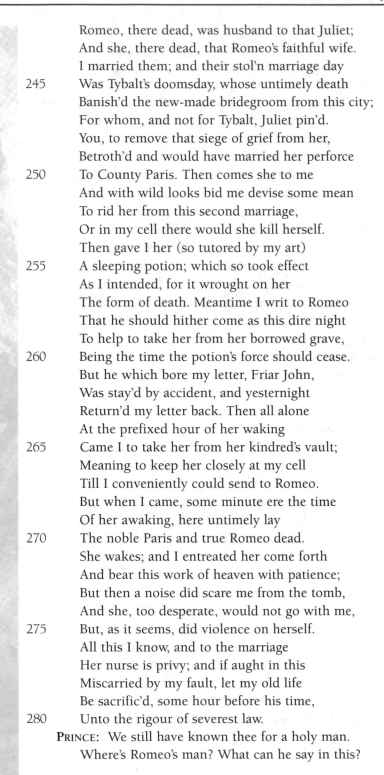

Romeo, there dead, was husband to that Juliet;
And she, there dead, that Romeo's faithful wife.
I married them; and their stol'n marriage day
245   Was Tybalt's doomsday, whose untimely death
Banish'd the new-made bridegroom from this city;
For whom, and not for Tybalt, Juliet pin'd.
You, to remove that siege of grief from her,
Betroth'd and would have married her perforce
250   To County Paris. Then comes she to me
And with wild looks bid me devise some mean
To rid her from this second marriage,
Or in my cell there would she kill herself.
Then gave I her (so tutored by my art)
255   A sleeping potion; which so took effect
As I intended, for it wrought on her
The form of death. Meantime I writ to Romeo
That he should hither come as this dire night
To help to take her from her borrowed grave,
260   Being the time the potion's force should cease.
But he which bore my letter, Friar John,
Was stay'd by accident, and yesternight
Return'd my letter back. Then all alone
At the prefixed hour of her waking
265   Came I to take her from her kindred's vault;
Meaning to keep her closely at my cell
Till I conveniently could send to Romeo.
But when I came, some minute ere the time
Of her awaking, here untimely lay
270   The noble Paris and true Romeo dead.
She wakes; and I entreated her come forth
And bear this work of heaven with patience;
But then a noise did scare me from the tomb,
And she, too desperate, would not go with me,
275   But, as it seems, did violence on herself.
All this I know, and to the marriage
Her nurse is privy; and if aught in this
Miscarried by my fault, let my old life
Be sacrific'd, some hour before his time,
280   Unto the rigour of severest law.
PRINCE: We still have known thee for a holy man.
Where's Romeo's man? What can he say in this?

BAL:　I brought my master news of Juliet's death;
And then in post[20] he came from Mantua
285　　To this same place, to this same monument.
This letter he early bid me give his father,
And threat'ned me with death, going in the vault,
If I departed not and left him there.
PRINCE:　Give me the letter. I will look on it.
290　　Where is the County's page that rais'd the watch?
Sirrah, what made your master in this place?
BOY:　He came with flowers to strew his lady's grave;
And bid me stand aloof, and so I did.
Anon comes one with light to ope the tomb;
295　　And by-and-by my master drew on him;
And then I ran away to call the watch.
PRINCE:　This letter doth make good the friar's words,
Their course of love, the tidings of her death;
And here he writes that he did buy a poison
300　　Of a poor 'pothecary, and therewithal
Came to this vault to die, and lie with Juliet.
Where be these enemies? Capulet, Montage,
See what a scourge is laid upon your hate,
That heaven finds means to kill your joys with love!
305　　And I, for winking at you, discords too,
Have lost a brace of kinsmen. All are punish'd.
CAP:　O brother Montague, give me thy hand.
This is my daughter's jointure,[21] for no more
Can I demand.
310　MON:　But I can give thee more;
For I will raise her statue in pure gold,
That whiles Verona by that name is known,
There shall no figure at such rate be set
As that of true and faithful Juliet.
315　CAP:　As rich shall Romeo's by his lady's lie—
Poor sacrifices of our enmity!
PRINCE:　A glooming peace this morning with it brings.
The sun for sorrow will not show his head.
Go hence, to have more talk of these sad things;
320　　Some shall be pardon'd, and some punished;
For never was a story of more woe
Than this of Juliet and her Romeo.

　　　　　　　　　　　　　　　　Exeunt omnes.

[20]*haste*

[21]*inheritance*

Vocabulary and Glossary

Prologue
mutiny – strife, rivalry
piteous – passionate

Act I, Scene I
colliers – people who dig or sell coals
valiant – brave
fray – brawl
partisans – weapons
pernicious – vindictive, wicked
beseeming – becoming
adversary – enemy, nemesis
ere – before
drave – drove
covert – thicket
augmenting – increasing
importuned – inquired, questioned
tyrannous – cruel, vicious
siege – the act of being encircled
ope – open
posterity – future generations

Act I, Scene II
merit – deserve
sirrah – sir
holp – helped
languish – persistent disease
heretics – people whose opinions differ from the official faith (Christianity)
scant – barely, hardly

Act I, Scene III
dug – teat, nipple
tetchy – touchy, oversensitive, irritable
trow – say
rood – crucifix
perilous – dangerous, hazardous
lineament – aspect, characteristic
margent – margin
endart – take flight and puncture like an arrow

Act I, Scene IV

prolixity – wordiness
Tartar – a warrior
lath – wood
burthen – burden
visage – face
wantons – tomboys
mire – mud
agate-stone – a stone with small figures cut into it
alderman – city ruler
traces – harnesses
gossamer – sheer, light filmy substance
benefice – secular lifestyle
ambuscadoes – traps
anon – promptly, soon
vile – wicked, heinous
steerage – direction

Act I, Scene V

nuptial – wedding ceremony
ward – dependent
rapier – a small sword
solemnity – festivities
disparagement – affliction, injury, harm
scathe – hurt, injure
princox – a rude, impolite boy
perforce – by necessity
choler – fury, anger
gall – detest, disgust
prodigious – threatening, ominous

Act II, Scene I

purblind – blind
Venus – Roman goddess of love and beauty
demesnes – domain, territory
invocation – the act of calling a superior for help

Act II, Scene II

vestal – symbolizing chastity
livery – dress
enmity – hatred
perjuries – falsehoods
Jove – chief Roman god, Jupiter
perverse – stubborn, difficult
ware – conscious of, aware
idolatry – worship
falconer – a hawk trainer
gyves – chains, shackles

Act II, Scene III

chequering – speckling, spotting
osier – tree of the willow family
shrift – confession
brine – tears
chid'st – scolds, reprimands

Act II, Scene IV

cleft – split
fantasticoes – gallants, cavaliers, suitors
roe – fish eggs
fishified – changed to a fish; Mercutio is making some sexual jokes here
dowdy – trollop, harlot, prostitute
hams – knees
ell – a measurement of forty-five inches
mar – hurt
troth – loyalty, devotion
bawd – whore, prostitute
lenten – made during Lent (a season in which meat was prohibited)
vexed – disturbed, troubled
shrived – forgiven
convoy – means of conveyance
prating – babbling
lieve – rather, "just as soon"
apace – swiftly

Act II, Scene V

lame – incapacitated, physically handicapped
heralds – couriers, messengers
feign – pretend
fie – a curse
beshrew – a mild curse
hie – leave
wanton – lusty

Act II, Scene VI
flint – stone for making fire
wanton – giving pleasure
blazon – compliment, glorify

Act III, Scene I
addle – jumbled
doublet – piece of men's clothing
zounds – derived from an oath "God's wounds" (swounds)
haunt – popular place
appertaining – relevant, pertinent
dry-beat – to beat, lash, wallop
pilcher – case or cover for a sword
passado – fencing term
effeminate – powerless, weak

Act III, Scene II
Phoebus – Roman god of the sun (Apollo)
Phaethon – son of Apollo
amorous – passionate, loving
garish – elaborate, pretentious
cockatrice – a mythological serpent said to have the ability to kill with a single
      look
weal – good fortune
corse – corpse
bedaub'd – covered, smeared
bower – surround
monarch – ruler
beguiled – fooled

Act III, Scene III
affliction – disaster
sack – attack
usurer – moneylender
digressing – departing

Act III, Scene IV
kinsman – relative

Act III, Scene V

jocund – joyful
asunder – apart
runagate – wanderer, nomad
dram – destructive, harmful potion
carrion – carcass
Prudence – typical name for a gossip
puling – whining
stratagems – plots, attacks
stealth – secret, concealed action
dishclout – dishcloth
twain – two

Act IV, Scene I

inundation – deluge, surge
pensive – melancholy
prorogue – postpone, suspend
arbitrating – settling, resolving
charnel-house – designated area for discarding bones of the dead
reeky – wretched, foul, vile
shanks – calves (parts of the human body)
surcease – stop

Act IV, Scene II

forsooth – in truth
gadding – lazily wandering, strolling
behests – orders, rulings
prostrate – lying flat
tush – "keep quiet"

Act IV, Scene III

orisons – prayers
receptacle – holding place

Act IV, Scene IV

quinces – fruits
trim – dress

Act IV, Scene V

aqua-vitae – alcohol (Latin: "water of life")
lamentable – wretched, woeful
martyr'd – sacrificed
confusions – chaos
dirges – sad songs played at funerals
troth – truth
pestilent – extremely offensive, dreadful

Act V, Scene I
presage – predict
apothecary – pharmacist
meagre – scrawny, slender
penury – poverty
caitiff – slave-like

Act V, Scene II
pestilence – disease

Act V, Scene III
obsequies – funeral rites
mattock – axe
ensign – sign, pennant
crimson – red
sunder – split; destroy
paramour – concubine, mistress
inauspicious – unlucky
sepulchre – vault, grave
contagion – disease
restorative – medication that brings life back
descry – find, uncover
ambiguities – mysteries, uncertainties
direful – horrible, awful

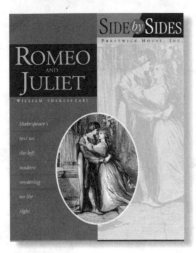